HOLIDAY

Minnesotans Remember
The Farmers' Holiday Association

edited by
DAVID NASS

foreword by
LYNDON JOHNSON

PLAINS PRESS
SOUTHWEST STATE UNIVERSITY
1984

Holiday copyright (c) 1984 by Plains Press, Southwest State University in Marshall, Minnesota. All rights reserved. No portion of this book may be reproduced without written permission except for selections contained in reviews or articles.

Typesetting by the Marshall (MN) *Independent*. Design by David Pichaske. Printing and binding by M & D Printers, Henry, Illinois.

1 2 3 4 5 6 7 8 9 10

Two editorial notes:

The interviews which comprise the bulk of this book were collected for the Minnesota Historical Society and Southwest State University by the following people: Jo Antonson, Joseph Amato, Maynard Brass, Art Finnell, Warren Gardner, Larry Jochims, Orville Miller, Mark Murdock, James Munson, David Nass, Diane Opp, Kathy Ramier and Dan Setterberg. The interviews are published here with the permission of the Minnesota State Historical Society and Southwest State University. Cover photo courtesy of the Minnesota State Historical Society.

Various sources print *Farmer's Holiday Association*, *Farmers' Holiday Association*, *Farmers Holiday Association*, *Farmer's Union*, *Farmers' Union*, and *Farmers Union*. I have settled on *Farmers' Holiday Association* because this spelling is used on Association letterhead in the Southwest State University History Center collection, and on *Farmers Union* because this spelling appears on Union publications of the 1930s.—D. P.

TABLE OF CONTENTS

Acknowledgments	v
A Note on Methodology	vii
The Farmers' Holiday: An Overview of Iowa and Minnesota	xi
Bibliography	xxix
Roy Peterson	1
Guy Lund	22
J. J. Kelly	38
William C. Goede	45
Vernon Runholt	55
William Nystrom	57
Percy Meehl	65
Ernest Johnson	73
Clint Haroldson	89
Gordon Thompson	105
D. W. Gold	108
William Johnson	115
Andrew Tkach	121
Louis Ebeling	127
Orville Tatge	131
Axel Mattson	137
John Engebretson	145
David Olson	149
Clarence Lund	163
John Reese	169
John Bosch	181

questions about what they thought the Holiday was trying to accomplish, how they went about it, and how successful they were. The careful reader will note that not all the participants necessarily saw things the same way.

In editing the original interviews care was taken to preserve the original character of each interview as much as possible. Language was changed only in cases involving clarity; for example, if a respondent spoke in a double negative in a sentence we would drop a word or phrase to insure a clear understanding. We did not drop colloquialisms or profanity. It was not our intent to make our respondents sound like English professors, but rather to return as much of the character of their speech as possible. The original tapes reveal some deep emotion that doesn't always come across as vividly in the printed word, but we did not include many comments indicating laughter, tears, or anger.

We tried to elicit comments and information from the interviewees without leading them to our conclusions. Our objective was to get our people going and hope they would tell an interesting story. We think they have and we hope you agree as you read these remembrances of a frustrating period in our nation's history.

D.N.
1/27/84

Farmers' Holiday demonstration in St. Paul, March 22, 1933. Photo courtesy Minnesota State Historical Society.

The Farmers' Holiday: An Overview of Iowa and Minnesota

The Farmers' Holiday was a farmers' protest movement of 1932-33 which flourished for a brief but memorable time in America's Middle West during the Great Depression. While the rest of the country marked the Depression with hobo jungles and Hoovervilles, the Heartland's memorials to the crash of 1929 were farm strikes — withholding food from market — and penny auctions. Though the national Farmers' Holiday never came close to realizing its stated goals, and it never wielded the sort of power it claimed to possess, the movement's impact on the state and local level in Minnesota and elsewhere in the Midwest was significant.

The movement had its genesis in the economic situation of the 1920's and the radicalization of the Farmers Union, one of the three largest farmers' associations in the United States. Farm credit had been a problem throughout the 1920's because the American farmer, particularly in the west central states, had borrowed heavily against the abnormally high produce prices and inflated land values of the war years and then, in the twenties, was faced with paying back these debts with products bringing pre-war prices. Most farmers were able to survive by floating new loans, but what had been a problem became a crisis with the crash of 1929, which saw prices plummet further and faster than anytime in American history. When the market finally bottomed out in June of 1932, corn sold for 10¢ a bushel, hogs sold for 3¢ a pound, and cattle for 5¢ a pound. Farmers burned corn for fuel and cattle sent to market did not even bring cost of transportation. The corn and livestock farmer was particularly hurt by this price decline, and the activist sentiment aroused by this condition in a part of the country where foreclosures were reaching epidemic proportions crystalized around the radical leader Milo Reno and the Iowa Farmers Union.[1]

The Farmers Union was responsible for most of the radical farm legislation introduced in the 1920's and 30's and the Iowa unit was the most radical of the state units. Reno had been an advocate of product-withholding efforts to raise prices since 1927; now, in the desperate cornbelt region — with no adequate legislative solution possible due to the conservative attitude of the Hoover Administration, the failure of the Cornbelt Committee and the decline of the farm bloc in the national legislature — his tactic had found its time and place. At the end of 1931, the National Farmers Union consented to Reno's withholding tactic. The organization implementing this tactic was the National Farmers' Holiday Association officially formed on May 3, 1932 at the Des Moines, Iowa fairgrounds. The new organization lost no time proclaiming a general withholding action to begin on July 4 and to continue for 30 days, or until cost of production prices were met.

While the Farmers' Holiday was in part a response to the unique economic situation among farmers during the 1920's and early 30's, it was also the last of a series of agriculturally based movements that spanned the years between 1870 and the New Deal. By the Civil War, with the introduction of the cash crop, necessary transportation to market, and the easy accessability of land in the Middle West, self-sufficient farming had for all practical purposes ceased to exist. Gone forever was the yoeman or the peasant villager; instead, the characteristic person to come out of rural America was "a harrassed little country businessman who worked very hard, moved all too often, gambled with his land and made his way alone."[2]

All the movements to come out of the era, despite their differences in tactics or objectives, had the same main goal: lessening the intense competitiveness, individualism and isolation of rural life. Whether the Granger's emphasis on fraternalism and education, the Populists'(Farmers' Alliance) and Non-Partisan League's political party activism, or the

Holiday with their pickets and penny sales demanding cost of production and mortgage relief, they were all seeking access to the comforts and security of a new American economic system which had long since passed agriculture by and left the farmer a seller in a buyer's market.

The Holiday was, in the opinion of several historians, the last chance to save the traditional family farm. Under the titular guidance and leadership of the evangelical and eccentric Reno, the Holiday began a series of activities that was to shock many elements of the populace, arouse bitter public debate, and at its height in the fall of 1932 and winter-spring of 1933, sway the legislatures of many state governments and elicit promises from presidential candidates.

The withholding strike, which finally began hesitantly on August 8, 1932 in Iowa, was the first of three such strikes called by the Holiday and took a course quite unplanned for by the national leadership. While Reno and the leaders planned that the withholding would be a peaceful one in which farmers would stay at home and keep their produce off the market as a political pressure tactic to bring about desired cost of production legislation, the farmers of Iowa had quite a different idea of what constituted a strike. Frustrated by 12 years of inadequate prices, the farmers of northwest Iowa took to the marketing roads armed with logs, thresher belts and nail-filled planks, determined to turn back produce from marketing centers. Peacefully if possible, by force if necessary.

On August 11 irate milk producers began to picket Sioux City, and by the 14th incoming produce was literally choked off by 1,500 strikers blockading the highways into the city. Strike-related violence began to escalate over the next several weeks, peaking on August 24 at Council Bluffs, when 500 farmers armed with rocks and clubs confronted amateur deputies armed with machine guns and tear gas. Though last-minute negotiations averted the calling in of standby national guard units and almost certain bloodshed, public fear of the blockade began to rise. The strike was never popular in Iowa, as evidenced by the Iowa Grange and Farm Bureau, the Farmers Union conservative sisters, which demanded that its members not only not participate in the strike but take active efforts to break it, and official appeals to the governor for troops to crush the picketing. Now with private and public patience wearing thin, a counter-assault began against the strikers. The nights of August 30, 31, and September 1 saw pitched battles between strikers and deputies on the outskirts of Omaha, and on August 30 fourteen strikers at Cherokee, Iowa, were wounded by shots fired from a speeding auto. Under pressure of further crackdowns and violence as well as the need for hard-pressed farmers to market goods, the Iowa and national Holiday leadership proclaimed on September 1 a temporary truce effective immediately.

The withholding had failed to raise the price received by farmers because the Holiday's base of support among Americans was too small to effect prices, even if they were sympathetic. Also strikers could not afford to hold produce for long periods in hard economic times and still meet basic expenses. But the spontaneous picketing actions of the Iowa farmers and the attendant violence had made the strike successful in a way that the leadership hadn't anticipated. While a peaceful withholding would have gone unnoticed, the turbulance in Iowa brought the plight of the farmers to the center of political attention.

No longer able to ignore the spirit of unrest present throughout the Midwest and alarmed at the possible spread of the potential anarchy that had shown itself during the brief strike, four midwestern governors held a conference in Sioux City on September 9 to address the farm problem. The governors were greeted by a parade of 5,000 farmers and were presented with the Holiday's demands, including state mortgage moratoriums putting a temporary stop to all foreclosures and state-enforced embargoes against the sale of farm products at less than cost of production. Although the resolutions and recommendations put forth by the governors at the end of the conference were mild and did not include any of the Holiday demands, a tone of political appeasement was set.

As the strike staggered along in Iowa, it acquired some vigor in Minnesota and caught national attention as the presidential candidates put forth promises to the activist farmers. By the end of September, Hoover had discussed with advisors a plan to raise commodity prices and announced that he had promoted discussions among eastern mortgage concerns and government agencies to stem foreclosure tide. In early October, Roosevelt, who had been evasive in speeches, promised Farmers Union leaders in a private conference that, if elected, he would make agriculture the number one priority and press for legislation providing cost of production and free financing of loans at low interest rates.

Bolstered by the accidently successful strike and the election of Roosevelt to the White House, the Holiday turned its attention to the more immediate problem of farm credit and foreclosures. Late in 1932 the Holiday became involved in an effort that would yield farmers their greatest success and raise the Holiday to the zenith of its influence.

To cut down on the tragic rate of real estate and chattel foreclosures that were ruining the lives of many midwestern families the Holiday relied on two methods. The first were County Councils of Defense composed of three to seven farmers who would meet with debtors and creditors and try to work out financial arrangements whereby foreclosure and dispossession could be avoided. If the first method failed, the farmers resorted to tactics of force and intimidation — physically blocking sheriff's sales or buying a farmer's belongings for a pittance and then returning them to him — that are the Holiday's most lasting legacy.

Perhaps because the penny sales and foreclosure stoppages offered the most immediate and attainable results, they attracted far and away the most support of any of the Holiday activities. In the winter and spring of 1933, the Upper Midwest was dotted with such stoppages. As usual northeast Iowa was the most noticeable. Martial law was declared in two Iowa counties by the governor on April 28 in response to pleas from local authorities after two incidents convinced them that the situation was beyond their control. In one instance, a judge hearing a foreclosure suit was abducted from his courtroom by an angry crowd and threatened with being hanged unless he swore to authorize no more foreclosures. In another, 800 farmers formed a flying wedge and, running, charged into the farmyard where a chattel mortgage was being foreclosed and subdued the fifty deputies assigned to guard the sale.

By March of 1933, seven states, either by executive request or by legislative action, had moved to restrain farm foreclosures. The Holiday was riding high, though precariously so. Though the national organization was able to hide its weaknesses through an aborted farm strike in May, a showdown with Roosevelt and the New Deal farm policy in November of 1933 would show the sparse support of the Holiday and mark its end as a national power.

The Holiday and the Farmers Union supported Roosevelt strongly in the 1932 election and had faith in his promises of low interest refinancing and cost of production, but the reality of the New Deal Program was quite different. While a form of low interest refinancing became law, the administration and Henry Wallace, the Secretary of Agriculture and former Iowa Farmers Union leader, opposed cost of production and instead instituted a crop allotment program to raise farm prices.

The allotment program, with its limits on production and volunteerism, infuriated Reno and segments of the Holiday leadership. The Holiday was based on the tenets that the farmers, as the backbone of the American economy, should be allowed to grow as much as he could, sell when he chose to, and receive cost of production plus a reasonable profit, and had supported compulsory legislation to insure this. To them the allotment was anathema and Wallace, a union man, a traitor.

There were rumblings of a general farmers' strike throughout the fall of 1933, and on the surface the Holiday appeared to be capable of promoting a damaging strike unless Wallace and the crop allotment program were dropped and a cost of production instituted. The fall prices had dipped to an all time low, and as a final testament to the Holiday's illusive power another governors conference was held on October 30, with the governors traveling to Washington to plead personally with Roosevelt to institute a cost of production program.

Roosevelt declined and on November 3 Reno proclaimed a farm strike effective immediately. The governors' worries were needless, however, as the strike proved most impressive in its weakness. Stopping a foreclosure at a county courthouse is one thing, but to threaten a popular president and alter a government program is quite another. The modern American farmer has always been by nature a practical individual rather than a social philosopher, preferring immediate financial returns to long-range planning, and with checks from the allotment in hand and more promises of help in the future the Holiday's support drifted away like the ghost it was.

This marked the end of the Holiday as a political force. Though it continued to exist until 1937, it was never a serious factor nationally again. With the end of the Holiday the trends toward consolidation and specialization, aided and abetted by the New Deal Farm Programs accelerated and the family farm continued to disappear.[3]

MINNESOTA FARMERS' HOLIDAY

While the majority of attention went to the more explosive and colorful Iowa movement, Minnesota was building the largest, longest lasting and most successful of the state Holiday units. More disciplined, organized and peaceful than its sister organization, the Minnesota Holiday's eventual fate was quite different.

When the Minnesota Association was formed July 29, 1932 in the gymnasium of St. Cloud Jr. High, the role of president and organizer went to John Bosch of Atwater, Minnesota, a man by birth and experience perfectly suited for the role. The self-educated son of an immigrant blacksmith, Bosch was the president of the strong Kandiyohi Farmers Union and, as a close associate of Milo Reno, had been named vice-president of National FHA. Bespectacled, diplomatic and an experienced organizer, Bosch preached restrained and "Ghandi-like" methods relying on the "moral persuasion" of the community to insure the eventual success of the Holiday. Under his leadership the Minnesota organization, with its broad-based leadership on the local, county, and state level, took on the appearance of a long-lasting, democratic political association which stood in contrast to the fraternal mob in Iowa.[4]

In a whirlwind organization during the month of August and early September, Bosch and trusted lieutenants canvassed Minnesota and particularly Southwest Minnesota to back up the Iowa strike. Living and traveling hand-to-mouth on donations, Bosch would launch his appeal to crowds of 500-1,000 people at county meetings.[5] Aided by Bosch's protestations of peaceful methods and possible ethnic factor which may have made Norwegian farmers more accepting to the Holiday's far-from-conservative program for American agriculture, the Holiday was able to establish strong organizations even in conservative Farm Bureau areas.[6]

By the time Minnesota went out to strike on September 21, it claimed organizations in 58 of Minnesota's 83 counties, but the figure is deceptive since many of these counties were organized in name only. The real strength of the Minnesota Holiday rested in west central and southwest Minnesota, particularly in a four county tier consisting of Chippewa, Lac Qui Parle, Yellow Medicine and Kandiyohi Counties. This area provided much of the Minnesota membership and leadership and was the spearhead of all the Minnesota Holiday actions. That the Holiday should be strong there is no surprise. The area was the home of the radical faction of the Minnesota Farmers Union and was particularly hard hit by the 20's. Its previous land values, among the highest in the state, had plummeted, and foreclosures occurred there at a rate surpassed in only a few counties statewide. Townships in this area reported strike sign-ups at rates of 80-90%; Kandiyohi County reported over 1,400 of its 2,500 owners and renters were members.

When the strike was inaugurated on September 21, with parades in several communities and fireworks in Willmar in Kandiyohi County, the tier of radical counties took the lead. The next day the Holiday completely closed off Montevideo to produce shipments by pickets in a blockade that was to last at varying levels of effectiveness for an entire month. Scattered picketing occurred throughout west central and southwest Minnesota, most notably at Worthington in Nobles County, where on the 19th local farmers had joined the strike early in sympathy with Iowa.

Public response, even in conservative areas, was remarkably tolerant. The general attitude of newspaper editorials was that the strike, although not likely to succeed, was a worthy effort and deserved the support of all farmers and those dependent upon the farmer for their existence. Picketers co-operated with county sheriffs, waylaid truckers played horseshoes with lounging strikers, local chamber of commerces signed pledges of support for the Holiday, and a

Worthington paper declared that the picketing and coverage was "priceless publicity and free advertising."[7]

In such an atmosphere the strike in Minnesota was marred by only a few unavoidable cases of minor blood-letting by fisticuffs, and a few punctured tires and broken windows. But as the strike wore on, serious opposition began to form against the Holiday.

Foremost and most serious was the growing public fear of violence. By early October roving bands of strikers from the four-county area and primarily from Montevideo began to fan out from their home base to bolster the strike in outlying areas and commit acts of vandalism in areas where they were not welcome. Confrontations between pickets and truckers and produce-marketing farmers began to increase as business returned to usual after an initial show of sympathy for the strike. But the two biggest blows to the Holiday were the shooting death of a young picketer, Nordahl Peterson, by an irate neighbor near Canby in Yellow Medicine County on October 5 and a riot at Howard Lake on the 12th between 500 strikers and 300 nonstrikers. The loss of life and confrontations between deputies and strikers caused many to reassess the strategy and tactics employed by the Holiday.

Upon the death of Peterson, several counties cut back on picketing, and one county dropped out entirely. With the increasing confrontations, newspapers began to wonder if the continuing of the farm strike had more to offer than "bloodshed and the turning of neighbor against neighbor."[8] The Minnesota Holiday leadership agreed and issued a call to end volunteer picketing and substitute an "observer" program in its place. The farm strike, although not officially suspended until early November, 1932, came to a quiet end on October 24 when 200 strikers in Montevideo, under the watchful eyes of 100 state troopers, turned back one last symbolic load of cattle from the local Hormel plant and peacefully dispersed.

Like the national movement, the anti-foreclosure actions of the Minnesota Holiday were the height of its power and influence. Local defense committees began forming in early December. An offer from a Minnesota Farm Bureau leader, the Holiday's arch enemy, to join forces and "take whatever actions necessary" to stop foreclosures boded well as the farmers plunged into what may have been the most effective anti-foreclosure effort in the nation.

In the first months of 1933 the Holiday stopped foreclosures by arbitration as well as foreclosure stoppages and penny sales in at least 20 counties in southwest and west central Minnesota. These extra-legal and illegal activities became so common, in fact, that foreclosure stoppages at four county seats on May first received only two paragraphs on the back page of only one local newspaper. Dispossession, if the farmer did not wish it, was unlikely.

However, the general impression of Depression foreclosures as instituted mostly by giant insurance companies, heartlessly throwing destitute families into the cold and being restrained single-handedly by determined crowds of brother farmers, is only partially true. Some farmers were so deeply and hopelessly in debt they wanted to be foreclosed, if they could be assured of not facing a difficiency judgement. Others, since mortgagers as a group were not completely insensitive to economic realities, worked out temporary rental agreements or sweetheart deals that allowed them to retain possession after foreclosure. Also, by the time such actions began in earnest in Minnesota, five major insurance companies had suspended foreclosure actions nationwide. It should be noted that while the Holiday did battle some insurance companies, it also battled financially hard-pressed, small-time investors and individuals.

The first foreclosure stoppage in Minnesota was at the Kandiyohi County Courthouse in Willmar, on the 25th of January, 1933. Eight hundred farmers gathered and caused the postponement of the sale of the homestead of Soren Hanson, a 70-year-old pioneer settler. After the stoppage, however, the mortgage holder refused to arbitrate and in what quickly became a battle of principle, the sale was stopped six times in succeeding weeks despite the death of Mr. Hanson in the interim.

The Holiday made its first real show of strength on January 28, when crowds ranging in size from 500 to 900 farmers stopped a half dozen sales in Lac Qui Parle, Yellow Medicine and Chippewa Counties, including the sale of one farmer being foreclosed by a lumber company for a $57 fence post bill.

The Holiday preferred to work privately through arbitration and was sensitive to possible damaging criticism of their interruption of the sacred creditor-debtor relationship and as such were at pains to point out that they were only trying to save good farmers done in by circumstances beyond their control. Keeping with this, when they averted a sale publicly they chose cases where the justice was most obvious. The strategy worked; public opinion, at worst, came to view the stoppages as a necessary evil of the time and many sheriffs were as solicitous as their legal duties would allow.

These were emotionally charged times, however, and though the Holiday kept as tight a lid as possible on extra-legal activites, on several occasions spontaneous actions in which passion overcame reason took place. In Lincoln County, three foreclosure sales were stopped by a crowd of 400 despite the impassioned pleas of the farmers involved that they wanted to be foreclosed.

In a west central county a farmer who decided to retire due to bad health worked out an equitable agreement to have his belongings sold at auction. Unfortunately the local paper ran the headline "Pioneer Farmer Forced From Farming," and when the unsuspecting creditor showed up for the sale he was greeted by 500 angry headline-reading farmers. Held hostage while the goods sold for a pittance, he was forced to flee — in legendary Holiday fashion — minus his pants and on four flat tires.

The stoppages and penny sales were effective as a means of addressing individual wrongs but they were also effective as a political pressure tactic. Bills and resolutions flooded the legislature and on the 25th of February, Governor Floyd B. Olson proclaimed a mortgage moratorium effective until May 1st. Though the moratorium was eventually ruled an unconstitutional exercise of executive power, legislation was soon to follow.

The proclamation and the subsequent legislation were the Holiday's greatest victory, and Olson's role has given him a somewhat undeserved reputation as patron of the Farmers' Holiday. Throughout the Holiday's peak, Olson's actions were those of a politician walking a tightrope, not a fearless champion of the common man. Olson did in fact proclaim a moratorium, but he did so only when politically safe. Publicly, Olson blamed the lack of legislation on a conservative senate and refused to call a moratorium because it was an "unprecedented and perhaps unconstitutional" exercise in executive power. Olson reversed his ground and used the powers only after the senate had passed a resolution demanding he take some kind of action.

The rest of Olson's actions take on a similar tone. He was steadfastly neutral and noncommital during the strikes, and when he took actions that were of concrete benefit to the farmers and the Holiday, he did so only when they were politically safe or to his own advantage.[9]

That he could remain a champion in the eyes of Holiday members was due to several factors. First, he maintained a close alliance with the Minnesota Leadership, who were lavish in their praise of him. Also, the Holiday had a tendency to see enemies all around them and, considering the hostile actions of some governors, Olson's neutral and sometimes contradictory public stances marked him as a friend. Last and most importantly he had a remarkable skill in convincing everyone that he was on their side, as evidenced by his performance at the 1932 governor's conference which drew praise from both the most pro-Holiday paper in the state for "his brave effort on the behalf of American Farmers" and the most anti-Holiday paper for "refusing to knuckle under to the bolshevist backed element of farmers."[10]

Despite some ominous rumblings from the public during the postponed May strike, the months following the mortgage proclamation were heady ones for the Minnesota Holiday. On March 22, 1933, upwards of 20,000 farmers descended on the capitol in St. Paul to show support for the Holiday legislative program. After holding a mass parade in front of the Capitol, the farmers swarmed the Capitol building and lobbied with legislators while, back home in Lac Qui Parle County, a delegation of Holiday wives halted a chattel foreclosure.[11] The summer and fall saw the Minnesota Mortgage Law upheld by the Minnesota Supreme Court and the formation of debt adjustment committees to scale down farmers' debts.

The Holiday was fully expecting a successful strike in the fall of '33, as evidenced by their plans for food depots to be established to feed communities during what they envisioned as a complete shutdown on the flow of produce, but public opinion had turned during the course of '33. Where the Holiday had previously met with support or neutrality, it was now met with outright resistance and hostility.

With benefits already accrued from the Roosevelt administration and the hope for more in the future, the public could see no reason for a strike which could not succeed in raising prices.

The Minnesota Farm Bureau, which had previously remained silent or discreet, condemned the strike in no uncertain terms, reflecting the feelings of those who feared strike violence or had always disliked the Holiday on principle.

LYNDON JOHNSON

Businessmen, particularly those in communities that had been picketed during the first strike, made public pronouncements that they would not sit idle while business flowed to nearby communities while they were shut off by picketing. But most importantly the farmers themselves turned on the strike.

Faced with the loss of their only source of income and possible damage to the co-ops they had worked hard to build, drought-stricken farmers voted overwhelmingly to keep co-op produce stations and creameries open. While the state executive committee claimed they could "live on bread, mush and milk for the duration of the strike rather than continue to live under present depressed farm conditions indefinitely," the majority of the people clearly would not.[12]

During the two-week strike, 13 counties saw the development of citizen protective leagues pledged to uphold the "farmer's right to market" and to do whatever was necessary to uphold this right. Faced with the overwhelming opinion of the populace, many counties withdrew from picketing in any form. Even in the strong tri-county area the strike was finished a week before it was officially ended on the 22nd.

However, the strike's weakness inspired the most desperate acts of the Minnesota Holiday. The Montevideo creamery was seized by the Holiday which, in siege-like atmosphere, used it as a communications center. On November 10th, 1933, in an action that received nationwide publicity, several thousand farmers descended on Marshall, Minnesota, slashed fire hoses, pelted police vehicles with rocks and disarmed the county sheriff, as they forced the closure of the Swift Plant there.

Though the fall of 1933 marked the end of the Holiday as a strike force, the Minnesota association remained strong, active, and healthy. With the decline of the Iowa unit, national leadership in the Holiday fell to Minnesota, and in May, 1936

John Bosch assumed the presidency upon the death of Milo Reno. The Holiday continued as a court of last resort for those cases of foreclosure that fell through legislative loopholes, including the expulsion of a federal marshall from a foreclosure auction in Chippewa County in 1936, but its primary role was political. Representing the interests of progressive farmers, the Holiday supported candidates and issues most likely to benefit the farmer and social justice. Despite flirtation with communist and socialist farm groups, including the use of communist organizers during a 1936 recruiting drive, the Holiday's politics remained relatively mainstream. In 1937, with the need for the emergency organization all but gone, the Holiday quietly merged back with the parent Farmers Union.

FOOTNOTES

1. Information on the Iowa and National Holiday taken primarily from John Shover's *Cornbelt Rebellion* (Urbana, 1965).

2. Richard Hofstadter, *The Age of Reform* (New York, 1955) p. 46.

3. The New Deal never provided much help for the small farmer and in fact did positive harm to the tenant farmer. This was not an accident, however, of a rushed economic recovery program. Many people influencial in the planning and implementation of the Agricultural Adjustment Act thought that there were too many farmers for the good of the economy, and the effect of the program reflected this. Theodore Saloutos, *The American Farmer and the New Deal* (Ames, 1982), p. XV

4. The Minnesota organization, because its members were recruited personally on the township level and the leadership kept in close contact with the rank and file, was able to co-ordinate and control its county organizations more than Iowa.

5. The Holiday was never a wealthy organization. Even at its peak in 1933 it was operating on a budget of $1,700 dollars a year in Minnesota. *Rock County Star*, Luverne, MN. July 21, 1933.

6. Ethnographic maps show a strong correlation between Norwegian influence and Holiday activities. Also ethnic Norwegians, especially in western Minnesota, had a traditional tendency to gravitate towards third party movements featuring agrarian radicalism such as the Populists and Non-Partisan League. A possible explanation is that the more newly established Norwegians in the West saw similarities between America's big business monopolies and the urban dominance they had known in Norway and were more prone to revolt. Jon Wefald, *A Voice of Protest* (Northfield, MN., 1971) pp. 34-44, 55-72.

7. *Nobles County Times*, Worthington, MN., September 22, 1932.

8. *Montevideo News*, October 14, 1932.

9. An example of this is his executive order which allowed county sheriffs, if there was danger of violence, to postpone foreclosure sales without risk of losing their office or forfeiting their bonding. While this act made it much easier for the Holiday to halt sales, it also greatly reduced the chance of violence and the possibility that Olson would be forced to

send in the national guard against farmers, an act which he rightly considered political suicide.

10. *Rock County Star*, September 16, 1932. *Windom Reporter*, September 15, 1932.

11. While women never had a significant official function in the Holiday, their contribution is summed up by John Bosch in a letter to a friend recalling a foreclosure stoppage. "We surely had a splendid bunch there that day. Nearly everyone had a rope or a fork and, more effectively, he had his wife along." Letter, John Bosch to E. H. Hillman, October 28, 1937, John Bosch papers.

12. *Montevideo News*, November 17, 1933.

BIBLIOGRAPHY

While the Holiday is the subject of numerous theses and dissertations, focusing primarily on the state and regional level, there are two published works dedicated to the national Holiday movement. The seminal work is John Shover's *Cornbelt Rebellion* (Urbana, 1965). Shover's work concentrates on the Iowa organization and the national president of the Holiday Association, Milo Reno. Shover, while sympathetic to the farmers' plight, is critical of the Holiday in his assessment of its political importance and, in particular, he makes short shrift of the Minnesota Holiday movement.

Everett E. Luoma's *The Farmer Takes a Holiday* (New York, 1967) stands in contrast to Shover's work. Less academic in nature, Luoma's book gives ample coverage to Minnesota and praises the Holiday in general. Particularly, he credits Governor Olson's pro-Holiday stance and the National Farm Holiday's role in the enactment of New Deal farm legislation.

Several other works also give substantial coverage to the Holiday. In their *Agriculture Discontent in the Middle West, 1900—1939* (Amdison, 1951), Theodore Suloutos and John D. Hicks devote several chapters to the farm strike and the conditions that led to it. Lowell Dyson's *Red Harvest* (Lincoln, 1982) is also noteworthy. Tracing the far from insubstantial involvement of communists in agricultural organizations from post-WWI to WWII, Dyson covers the national and Minnesota Holidays as well as the role of John Bosch in keeping the Holiday from becoming a communist front in its last years. Also available is Dale Kramer's *The Wild Jackasses: The American Farmer in Revolt* (New York, 1956).

For works on individuals involved with the Holiday and the New Deal, see George Meyer, *The Political Career of Floyd B. Olson* (St. Paul, 1951); Roland White, *Milo Reno, Farmers Union Pioneer* (New York, 1941); Edward and Fredrick Schapsmeier, *Henry Wallace of Iowa; the Agrarian Years,*

1910—1940 (Ames, 1968) and Theodore Saloutos, *The American Farmer and the New Deal* (Ames, 1982).

For works relating to previous rural protest movements, see D. Sven Nordin, *Rich Harvest: A History of the Grange, 1867—1900* (Jackson, 1974); Robert Wiebe, *The Search For Order, 1877—1920* (New York, 1967); John Hicks, *The Populist Revolt* (Minneapolis, 1931); Richard Hofstadter, *The Age of Reform: From Bryan to F.D.R.* (New York, 1955) and Robert Morlan, *Political Prairie Fire* (Minneapolis, 1955).

Especially useful for the Minnesota Farm Holiday movement is a collection of primary sources housed at the Southwest Minnesota Historical Center, Southwest State University, Marshall, Minnesota.

CHRONOLOGY ON AMERICAN AGRICULTURE POST-WORLD WAR I

1918-19: Golden years of American Agriculture. Prices and land values abnormally high.

1920: Foreign market collapses as Europe returns to production after devastation of World War I. Prices fall to pre-war level and farmers who had borrowed against boom prices face credit problems.

1921: The Farm Bloc, a coalition of Midwestern congressmen and senators, organized to promote legislation favorable to agriculture. The Grange, Farm Bureau, and Farmers Union support the Farm Bloc.

1925: Cornbelt Committee formed at urging of Farmers Union: A loose confederation of 24 farm associations, the Committee sought to bring about farm legislation at the Federal level, most notably the McNary-Haugen Act.

1928: McNary-Haugen Act, which would have guaranteed farmers a fair price based on 1910-14 levels, vetoed for second time by President Coolidge.

1929: Great Crash, which sent farm prices spiraling downward to all-time low. Farm credit becomes crises situation and the Cornbelt Committee became dominated by Farmers Union radicals—led by Milo Reno—who demanded immediate cost of production.

1930: Radicals, who favored political action and produce withholding if necessary, assume leadership in National Farmers Unions.

1931: The Cornbelt Committee comes to an end as moderates secede en masse. Final crippling price decline hits cornbelt region of United States.

January, 1932: Milo Reno begins formation of direct action organization to press for Farmers Union demands.

May 3, 1932: National Farmers' Holiday Association formed at DesMoines, Iowa.

July 29, 1932: Minnesota Holiday Association formed at St. Cloud meeting.

August 8, 1932: Farm strike begins in Iowa, predominantly in northwest section.

August 14, 1932: Sioux City closed to produce shipments by 1500 picketers.

August 24, 1932: Battle of Council Bluffs.

August 30, 1932: 14 pickets at Cherokee, Iowa wounded by gunfire.

September 1, 1932: Temporary truce called by Iowa leaders.

September 9, 1932: Midwestern Governors Conference in Sioux City to consider farm problem.

September 21, 1932: Minnesota joins withholding; picketing in scattered areas of southwest and west central Minnesota.

October 5, 1932: Nordahl Peterson shot and killed while on picket duty near Canby, Minnesota in Yellow Medicine County.

October 12, 1932: Riot between pickets and non-pickets at Howard Lake, Minnesota.

October 20, 1932: Minnesota leadership requests end to volunteer picketing and instituion of observer program in its place.

November 1932: Strike temporarily suspended nationwide: Reno request county organizations begin forming councils of defense to deal with foreclosure problems.

December, 1932 - May 19, 1933: Foreclosure stoppages and penny sales occur throughout midwest as Holiday reaches high point of its strength and influence.

January 21, 1933: First of many foreclosure stoppages in Minnesota occurs at Willmar courthouse, Kandiyohi County.

January, 28, 1933: Foreclosure sales stopped in Yellow Medicine, Chippewa and Lac Qui Parle Counties.

February 25, 1933: Governor Olson announces moratorium proclamation. State legislature follows with moratorium law.

March 22, 1933: Farmers march on State Capitol at St. Paul.

March, 1933: Franklin D. Roosevelt inaugurated and appoints henry A. Wallace as Secretary of Agriculture. National Holiday Convention calls strike for May if acceptable legislation is not adopted by then.

April 27, 1933: Judge kidnapped from courtroom in LeMars, Iowa and threatened with lynching by angry crowd. On following day in neighboring county farmers subdue 50 deputies at forced sale.

April 28, 1933: Angered by Wallace and the administration's allotment plan, national Holiday Convention votes to strike on 13th of May.

May 12, 1933: realizing how damaging the incidents at Iowa had been to public opinion and that the spring was a poor time to have farmers strike, Reno excedes authority and calls off strike.

Summer 1933: After slight recovery, market prices fall sharply and clamor for Wallace's resignation increases.

October 30, 1933: Governors meet once again in Sioux City and travel to Washington for personal meeting with President Roosevelt to accept mandatory cost of production. Roosevelt responds politely but negatively.

November 3, 1933: Reno calls national strike effective immediately. Response, even in Iowa, weak.

November 3, 1933: Minnesota joins strike. Public response hostile and in course of next several weeks "Citizen Protective Leagues" begin to spring up in response to farm strike.

November 10, 1933: Farmers disarm sheriff and cause closing of Swifts plant in Marshall, Minnesota. Railroad bridges burned in Iowa.

1934-1937: With Iowa membership dwindling, leadership in national organization flows to large, healthy Minnesota association. Orientation switched from direct action to politics.

1936: Bosch assumes presidency of Farmers' Holiday Association upon death of Reno. Holiday attempts merger with United Farm League and other far left splinter farm organizations. Merger falls through and Holiday makes its peace with the New Deal and supports Roosevelt for president instead of William Lempe of North Dakota.

1937: Holiday quietly rejoins the Farmers Union.

Governor Floyd Olson. Photo courtesy Minnesota State Historical Society.

Peterson, Roy
S216

Roy Peterson was born in Beardsley. He moved to Benson in 1924. He has been the Oak Grove Dairy distributor since 1952. He also has his own dairy herd. He was active in the Farmer Labor Party and Farm Holiday Movement. Roy attended the FHA state convention where he represented Swift County.

Then would you say the Farmers' Holiday Movement cooperated with either of these two parties or groups [The Non-Partisan League and The Farmer-Labor Party]?

The Farmers' Holiday Movement was made possible because they had the understanding that they'd gotten in economics. The Non-Partisan League and the Farmer-Labor Party did a terrific job in the early twenties of educating the people as to why we had the conditions we had, what caused them and what would remedy them. And the Holiday Association didn't attack the symptoms, they attacked the cause.

You're saying then that the Farmers' Holiday Movement was kind of a smaller part of the party?

It was a small thing in the beginning, but it caught on so much more quickly in Minnesota because the farmer understood the situation, the truth of the situation.

What was that situation?

The situation was that up until 1920 we had been an agricultural nation and then we started becoming an industrial nation. They wanted cheap labor in the cities and by forcing the farmer off the farm, that made a pool of unemployed that would beat down prices so the manufacturer wouldn't demand high prices. And the farmer was caught in the middle. He was supposed to produce the food cheaply and compete with one another, and they fooled a lot of them for a time.

The Farmers' Holiday Movement originated in Iowa?

It originated in Iowa. Milo Reno, who was state president of the Farmers Union, mentioned several times that if the farmer would go on strike like the working man that he would get somewhere. Finally sombody challenged him, and they said they thought it was time for the farmer to go on strike and they started a strike. It grew so fast and so big here that it got out of Milo Reno's control, in fact. He became national president of the Farmers' Holiday, but he could not control his local units. It was organized in counties in most states. And that's the difference between the NFO and the Farmers' Holiday Movement. In the NFO if we wanted to do something we had to consult Oren Lee Staley, the head of the NFO, and if he turned thumbs down on it we weren't supposed to do it. In the Holiday Movement we knew what was to be done, and we did it and we didn't need any sanction from Milo Reno or anybody else; we went ahead and got the job done. It worked real good.

That's interesting. You said that the Farmers' Holiday Movement was organized on a county basis?

Each county set up a unit and elected officers.

So there was a Swift County unit?

Swift County unit and Kandiyohi, Renville, Chippewa, Lac Qui Parle Counties. They were the first ones. I think probably the most militant and the most successful.

This was in 1932?

It started in '32.

And it lasted until about when?

After Roosevelt got in and they got a farm program, the farmer started to get on his feet a little. We lost membership because there wasn't a definite need for it. Actually in one sense of the word, you might say it had performed its function. And really I don't like to say it shouldn't, it should have ceased to have to exist. But we didn't have that, the farmers were so desperate. Due to the Holiday, Roosevelt called Milo Reno and told him to call off these farm strikes. And Reno told him he couldn't stop it any more than he could stop a prairie fire. Roosevelt said, "Then actually do we have a revolution?" Well I don't know, what else could you call it? It was a young revolution. God-fearing, respecting, law-abiding farmers were defying the law-enforcement authorities and meeting them in some cases with pitchforks and shot guns, although they didn't have any violence here in Minnesota in Swift County. The law-enforcement officers in Minnesota seemed to be pretty much in sympathy with the farmers, so we didn't have trouble that way.

How many people in Swift County were involved?

There were a little over 1900 people—farmers in Swift County at that time, and now it's way down. We had 1700 and some paid-up members. Some townships had every farmer a member of the Farm Holiday. But over 90% of the people belonged—farmers.

And they were trying to stop foreclosures?

95% of the farms in Swift County, and I assume that was true in many other counties, were mortgaged to the hilt for all they were worth then. And the insurance companies demanded their interest and their money. In some cases they had to pay interest for two or three years. Insurance companies had to pay the taxes because the farmers just didn't have any money. And they wanted either that paid up or they wanted foreclosures. And they were taking these farms away from these farmers, and these farmers had no place to go. At first, before Roosevelt got in, there wasn't much relief and they had their backs to the wall. They just fought back. It's the only thing they could do: either fight back or give up.

And how did they fight back?

By preventing the sheriff from selling the farms. At first when we started to do that there'd be two or three thousand at a courthouse to stop the sheriff. It kept taking less and less until finally it dawned on the insurance companies. They learned the hard way that we wouldn't permit these foreclosures. So they would write to the secretary or the president of the Holiday in each county and ask them if they could foreclose on a certain farm and give them the details. We had a debt adjustment committee in each Holiday and they would size up the situation, and if they thought there was any possible chance and if the farmer wanted to stay on his farm and try and make it they would tell, turn thumbs down on the foreclosure and insurance company or holding agency would not foreclose on it. They'd go along with them.

Wow.

No, this become so effective that the powers that be didn't like it, so they had the governor of each state set up a debt adjustment committee. In Minnesota Floyd B. Olson was the governor and the farmers had helped elect him and the laborers, and he knew which side his bread was buttered on. The thinking among these loaning agencies was that the governor of the state would be conservative and was to enforce the law; he was commander-in-chief of the National Guard and he was to enforce the law and he would do this. But there they reckoned without Floyd B. Olson. Immediately he contacted the Holiday in each county and he says, "Who do you want on these debt adjustment committees?" And they invariably named the same people that were functioning in the Holiday, doing the same thing but without official appointment from the governor. He would appoint who the Holiday told him. Sometimes he would add a banker, but there were enough farmers on the committee so they could handle this banker if he were too conservative.

I take it Olson was kind of a unique governor?

He was a unique governor; he was a dynamic, silver-tongued orator. He'd been mentioned for the presidency had his life not been cut short in his prime. He had cancer and died in Rochester of cancer. He was a good friend of Roosevelt's and he had a terrific following.

It sounded like he really tried to understand the farmer.

Oh he did. His father was a railroad man and he understood unions. This is getting off the track a little, but during a truckdriver's strike in the 30's when Local 574 went on strike, Minneapolis was an open town. And they fought that thing through, and the governor didn't protect the employers any more than he did the employees. They defied him to call out the national guard, which he did, but the guard didn't stop the strike. And as a result since then at that time, Minneapolis became a closed town. It's a union town, and it still is. But it was a terrific battle. As I recall, the first thing he did when he called out the militia, he fired the head of the national guard, because Dayton's and Donaldson's were entertaining him every Sunday and between times to boot, wining and dining him. And he said Olson's reason was he didn't think that he could be impartial in the Guards, in his enforcement of the law. So he fired him and they combed the constitution with a fine comb trying to find out if the governor had authority to do that, and he did have authority to do it. So it worked out good for the working man.

It sounds like there was a lot of support for Floyd Olson. Back to Swift County and the Farmers' Holiday Movement: were there meetings held and officers elected and that sort of thing?

We had meetings every month and oftener if necessary. In the occasion of an emergency, why sometimes we'd have a meeting a week, even two meetings depending on whatever the situation demanded.

How did you publicize your meetings?

The local papers gave us good publicity, real good publicity. Even the *Minneapolis Trib*, when we'd elect officials they would have that on the front page, who was elected in different counties. They gave us good publicity. As I remember, there was a guy at the head of the Swift County — he was only in a few months — the most effective and the best by far, outstanding chairman we had was Frank Perry, Dr. Frank Perry, a veterinarian from Appleton. Great big Irishman. Very impressive looking man, dignified. Sort of a gruff voice. He had the ability to say a whole lot with just a few words. He should have been an attorney because he had a terrific mind and he was just a natural leader of the people; they all looked up to him. Bankers respected him.

I might add this, that the farmer could only get loan money for his farm to pay off his mortgage at the Federal Land Bank. At that time insurance companies and loaning agencies wanted nothing more to do with farm loans because they'd been delinquent so long. So Roosevelt was instrumental in liberalizing the policy of the Federal Land Bank so that farmers could get money in order to pay off these mortgages. That was a bone of contention because sometimes these companies really wanted these farms, and it took a little while to get these farms appraised by the Federal Land Bank. I know in our county, in many counties, I'm sure most of them, there was a certain amount of money, said they could have that much money. Well immediately the insurance companies thought they'd get it all. In order to keep these farmers on their farms, the businessman, the butcher and baker and so forth, implement dealer, they had trusted these farmers and let them run up bills in order to keep them in business and to keep themselves in business. They wanted business. So the Holiday debt adjustment committee would say these businessmen don't have any legal right to collect this out of these companies that have the mortgages, but they have a moral right to collect it. We are going to see that part of this money that the Federal Land Bank will loan these farmers goes to pay the butcher and the baker and so forth. So it did help the businessman. It was a fair thing. These insurance companies didn't have a heart. Pardon me.

You mentioned that Frank Perry was the president.

Frank Perry, and I should mention some other names. George Hacker was secretary, an outstanding man, died a few years ago of cancer. He and Frank Perry died about the same time, but George was very much respected throughout the whole county. He was an honest man, upright man and a man that wasn't afraid to say what he thought. My dad had tremendous respect for him, and George did for my father. My father and he were officers and he [Mr. Peterson's father] was vice president when Frank was president, and those three worked together. Frank Perry and the local banker and George Hacker and sometimes my father would go down to the Federal Land Bank with these farmers that owned these farms that were applying for these loans. One summer Frank told me in three months he made 38 trips to the Federal Land Bank. He says, "I come in there so often," he says, "they say 'hello Frank' when I come in." He was comical, you know.

Sounds like he must have been a strong man too; he'd get so much cooperation.

He commanded even his enemies, they respected him. He should have been an attorney. A local here, John I. Davis, said he wished Frank had a, or was an attorney. He says, "He could make the bullets and I could fire them."

Are there any big incidents that happened in Swift County in relation to foreclosing or the Farmers' Holiday?

Really we had no violence here. There was a lot of enthusiasm in those times. As I say farmers didn't have any money. When now we want to go to town or want to go to Minneapolis, we jump in our car and go, but if we went to another town or another county to help — which we often did — why we'd always take a carload. Nobody went unless he took his neighbor with him, because in order to save gasoline they couldn't afford each to drive. And it promoted friendliness and neighborliness, I think. Some of that was lost now in our modernization, so-called progress.

I think last time we talked you mentioned you were going to Chippewa County quite a bit to help them out.

Chippewa County had some outstanding leaders also. Harry Haugland just passed away about a year ago. Was a terrific man, good speaker and very sincere, very forceful, respected. Elmer Bolman was another one. Henry Wolf, Laura Wolf his wife, was a great fighter, was a militant woman, a brilliant woman she was. They've all passed away. There was a Burle Porter also. I might say that over at Marshall that the meat plant, packing plant, there was a strike and the Holiday went over to help them and there was a little violence there. They got their local fire boys out, the powers that be did, and the Holiday proceeded to chop their hoses with axes and made them ineffective in a short time. At a sale over at Ortonville where they were taking the personal property away from a widow — Burle Porter was there, Frank Perry from this county, quite a few guys — and they decided this widow should keep her things. So they started bidding cheap, maybe ten cents for something that would have a value of several hundred dollars and so forth. One guy, he stepped up and he bid 25 dollars on it; he didn't belong to Holiday obviously, and Burle Porter stepped up to him and he says, "I think you bid a little high," he says; "that should have been 25 cents." And the deputy sheriff there immediately pulled his gun and shot him in the eye. And it was a . . . .

The Farmer's Holiday man?

Yes. It was a tear gas gun. And Burle went down like a stuck hog. They also had the patrol, highway patrol there and they tipped their car upside down and took the guns away from them. Told them if they'd come back and be gentlemen they could have their guns. Burle lost the sight in the eye; he never had the sight of that eye, and he died. That's about the only violence we had here. But they also won that battle. The widow kept all her property, and I think the sale come to 15 dollars and the Holiday paid that and she kept her property. An the local banker was holding the sack in that case.

Last time you talked about an incident with the U.S. marshall.

The insurance companies decided that the farmers elected the sheriffs in these rural area, and they said whoever paid the piper could call the tunes. The farmers paid for electing the sheriff, and they could control the sheriff, and the sheriff was soft. So there was another area and the usual manner of foreclosing: notice was served on the person who was being foreclosed on by the sheriff, was given an official copy that in six weeks this place would be sold. That had to appear, that advertisement had to appear six times in the county paper. So everybody knew of it. And there was another way to foreclose, and that's by federal court order. No advertising. Nobody knew it except the one being foreclosed on and the ones that are doing it.

They tried that. Union Central had a loan on a half a section in Chippewa County, and they made the statement that there was going to be inflation and they wanted that half a section. And the owner of the farm applied for a Federal Land Bank loan that it would be due, the money would be available in about ten days, but Union Central wanted that farm. They got the U.S. marshall at Mankato to order the farm sold, the U.S. marshall in Chippewa County. And immediately word come out on the grapevine that the federal marshall was going to foreclose on this particular farm and all the farmers in this area were requested to come down there to Chippewa to greet this federal marshall and acquaint him with the facts of life the way we understood them out here. So it was right in threshing time, and they used good psychology. If ever a farmer don't want to leave his work or his employment it's in threshing when the weather is ideal, and they chose that time. They thought he wouldn't quit threshing. Locally around Benson several rigs shut down. After we got half way to Montevideo we saw that every rig was abandoned, sitting by a straw pile; they had stationary straw threshers in those days. And there were five or six thousand people there to greet the marshall. I was kind of mad at the marshall, but I felt sorry for him because that man aged twenty years in about twenty minutes. He was afraid. I never seen a man so frightened as he was. And after the deal was all over, why he called this judge and the judge said it had to go through. Harry Haugland talked to him and he understood and told Harry in conversation that it wouldn't go through, so he told the marshall to call it off.

And then we asked him to come upstairs. He didn't want to go, but they insisted he come, and we had a meeting there. John Bosch, the state president of the Farmers' Holiday, says, "Now I want you to listen carefully, Mr. Marshall. Take back, make mental notes and take back what these farmers say to you to get the temper of the people here!" And he says, "We didn't want any violence to come to you and none did." And then he told the people we mustn't hold any resentment to this marshall because he's merely doing his duty for which he's paid. He admitted that it was a raw deal that they couldn't wait another ten days for their money, the insurance company, but he had to do his duty. So several farmers spoke, and then my dad asked for the floor. And I guess he was something like in Iowa, they never knew what he was going to say. Because John Bosch and Allenson Peterson wanted the floor, and he says, "I don't know what he's going to say."

And my father told him, he says, "You're defending a U.S. marshall and he says he doesn't like to do this but it's his duty and he detached it, and we shouldn't hold any ill will to him. I don't want any physical harm to come to him, but if his job belittles him, why he has the privilege of resigning. He wouldn't need to have this job to do these disagreeable tasks. There's other ways of making a living than being U.S. marshall." It got a lot of applause. O.B. Augeson from Willmar was there, and he printed the *West Central Tribune* and he quoted my father verbatim on that speech.

Who did you say that was?

O.B. Augeson.

That wasn't Victor Lawson?

Victor Lawson's nephew. Vic was the uncle. Maybe Vic was living at that time. I don't know about O.B. was there and he give a speech too. Have you met O.B.?

No.

Little vigorous active guy. Drinks enough coffee to kill a hundred people. Well, I've elaborated a lot; maybe this is getting too lengthy. You'll have to cut out the unimportant things.

I think this is really interesting and I'm still going to ask some more questions on the Farmers' Holiday.

O.K. If I can answer them.

Were there state-wide conventions or regional conventions?

We had state-wide conventions, we had national conventions. I only attended one which Huey Long was the main spokesman.

The governor of Louisiana?

He was U.S. Senator from Louisiana. He had been governor. He made Standard Oil pay for a big bridge there, one of the longest bridges in the world. They said they'd quit pumping oil and leave Louisiana, but they built the bridge and they didn't quit pumping oil.

You were a representative from this region to that?

From Swift County that's right.

About what year was that?

That was 1935. It was reported that Huey Long . . . . He was a character, a powerful individual.

What sort of things did he say at the Farmers' Holiday Movement? I really can't see him at a convention for you.

Well he was making it, he was a politician. And in my mind he had all the earmarks of a fascist dictator. He wanted to guarantee everybody a $5,000 income. I don't know if you was supposed to work for it or not. I'm assuming you're supposed to work for it. He wrote a book, *Every Man a King*. And Huey come up the hard way. He had terrific wit a brilliant mind, but I was afraid of the man. He had fascist tendencies and the earmarks of a dictator. He was ambitious politically.

What sort of things did he say at this convention?

Well I'm getting old and senile, and my memory isn't too

good. He said about the things like today Senator Humphrey would say. He said the things that people in that organization wanted to hear at that time. He sensed that. He praised us for stopping foreclosures and for fighting for the cost of production and uniting so we wouldn't have these foreclosures. Cost of production with a reasonable profit was what we wanted. And he said mainly what we wanted to hear. He made a good impression on the average person. I enjoyed hearing him thoroughly.

What was the convention like otherwise? Was it just keynote speeches?

No, they were planning on bills to introduce in the Congress and things to straighten out this depression that agriculture was in. They were in a depression according to M.W. Thatcher, who was head of the G.T.A. [Grain Terminal Association] and he said a mouthful. It's been farm-bred and farm-led, and also Thatcher said farm prices are made in Washington D.C. and we were aware of this.

The resolutions that you drew up and wanted to become laws dealt with the cost of production with a little, with reasonable profit.

That's right. It was to keep the family farm, and laws being passed were to the end that they would insure, guarantee that the family farmer could stay on the family farm. And to us this was what made America. First they got the railroads in here. In order to get the railroads the government gave them every other section of land to get them in here. Then they gave the people a right to file on a claim; for very little money they could get a quarter section of land, but they had to live on it five years and put up a certain amount of buildings. And this country was no good until we got people in here. To have people you had to have railroads, and the government realized this. Now they're doing it in reverse. They're cutting the railroads off. One farmer . . . well, I've got neighbors that farm

3,000 acres of land, and I don't blame them for doing it. But we're eliminating the people. And where're they going to go? The cities already have their problem with too many people, and I don't think we know how to pile up people by the hundreds and thousands and even millions in one concentrated area and live a natural good life. I think we can live that way out here. We're doing just the reverse of what the government did. The biggest asset to me that America has is our people. Without the people in this area, I don't know; to me it's a ruination of America, because we have no place for them to go. Now they always said, "Get an education." Fine. I wish I'd had six or eight years of college; I sure could have used it. But now I have many friends and all, people that went into teaching. They got their B.A. and some of them their Master's Degree to go in education. They can't get jobs. A neighbor boy applied for a job in a little town. He wants to teach English. He majored in English and Speech. They wrote back and told him they had 1,600 applications. I asked him if he got the job and he said, "What do you think?" Where're we going to put these people?

So you say the Farmers' Holiday wanted to keep the smaller farm families there instead of the larger farm operations?

That's right.

Were there any requirements for joining the Farmers' Holiday Movement? You said earlier that the businessmen were sympathetic, even though they weren't members.

There was a requirement you had to have 50 cents at first, and then they got real expensive and they had to pay a dollar a year to belong. That, and you had to be a bona fide farmer.

What do you mean by bona fide?

The major source of your income was supposed to come from the farm.

Did you have many people who rented land to other people members of the movement?

There were some renters at that time, and they all would have been renters or else on relief had it not been for the Holiday. John Bosch — who was president of the Farmers' Holiday, Minnesota Farmers' Holiday, who later went into insurance and became I understand a millionaire — he said at a meeting of the Holidays, the Holiday Association saved the American farmers about a billion and a half dollars in Minnesota. To me it was the most successful, perhaps the only successful farm organization the farmer ever had.

You were pretty active, I take it, in just going to these meetings.

I took part in all the discussions. Been one of my troubles in life: I've been talking when I should be listening. The only time you learn is when you listen. And maybe I didn't listen enough, but everybody could have their say. These meetings were very orderly, very democratic. Frank Perry was a terrific chairman. If anybody got off the subject, he could get them on in a hurry. And we had a good meeting. I was on several committees.

Did you meet, well, at different places throughout the county or in parks or where?

We'd generally meet in the courthouse here.

You mean in the courtroom?

Yes, in the courtroom, where we defied the law. The county courthouse was always open to us. In case of court, when the court was in session, they don't permit any meetings, because it entailed too much work for the janitor, but we could always meet in the basement. When it got just to be a few people, they met in the sheriff's office, when they were stopping foreclosures. Just a half a dozen Holiday members would come in.

They got so powerful that it only took half a dozen at a time?

Yes, they realized that they couldn't do these things. The company did. They had to recognize its [the Holiday's] authority, whether illegal . . . as it was, they called it illegal. I recall one time I drove for my dad. It was a blizzard and we met in the back of the Swift County Bank and with the banker. Floyd Olson put him on this debt adjustment committee. And there was four lawyers from Wheaton: Murphy, Johanneson . . . no, two from Wheaton — Frank Murphy and Johanneson — two lawyers from Minneapolis. They wanted this land this farmer had. They represented the insurance company; I don't recall what insurance company. Every once in a while lawyers in Minneapolis, they'd say, "Well why is it that in Swift County they put so much heat on us attorneys?" Pretty soon Frank Murphy would make that statement, and they all made it several times.

And finally Frank Perry, who was also chairman of this debt adjustment committee he says, "You've asked this question many times," he says, "and nobody saw fit to answer."

"But," he says, "I think it's time that, do you want me to answer it?"

"Ya"

He says, "Are you sure?"

"Yes. We want to know why they put so much heat on us in Swift County."

"We're just preparing you lawyers for your hereafter," he says. You know the meeting hadn't gone anywhere until then. And then, you know, they looked up and they was kind of mad because he indicated they was going to a place where the temperature was higher than it was in Swift County, and they saw the humor of the situation. They started to laugh and from then on the meeting went good. They started to get places. The farmer kept his farm, incidentally. It really wasn't incidentally, it was intentionally, intended that way. But he had that sense of humor. I know at many meetings they weren't getting anywhere and the air, you know, it was real tense; you could just feel it in the air. And Frank would make some remark like that, and everybody would relax, and they'd kind of forget their differences, and the meeting would go on. This is an ability that ... it's a gift I think. I don't think you can learn it in high school or college or anywhere else. You have to have this. Maybe it can be developed some. But it's interesting to watch these different people. Some people are natural leaders and some are followers.

It sounds like the Farmers' Holiday was very strong in this area ....

It was strong.

Then you said it was that there was no longer a need for it?

The farmers, they started pay. They had these corn and hog contracts which was part, and the ever-normal grainary. So the farmer was able to chisel out a bare living and he was happy too, because he'd gone through such tough times. So they were keeping their farms, and then World War II was in the offing and actually we didn't need the Farmers' Holiday. It had a lot of political weight. Gee whiz. A terrific...you know most of the farmers belonged, and the rural vote in Minnesota can swing an election. Could at that time. Now the urban centers have gotten so big it isn't as big a factor.

What's the ever-normal grainary?

That was part of Henry Wallace's farm program when he was

Secretary of Agriculture under FDR. It was that we should have a strategic supply of grain in case of lean years. He quoted the Bible on Joseph when he had seven good years and he filled up the grainaries. Then they had lean years. He saw this in a dream evidently. I'm not an authority on the Scripture, so I better not go into that. But anyway, it was to insure a supply of grain, and that the farmer got paid a decent price for it. The farmer could borrow on his grain from the government. There was a floor placed under the price. He could borrow a certain price, while if the elevator or the markets wouldn't pay that price, they'd just store it in these grainaries. They had these grainaries on their farms, and keep it [the grain].

In order to buy this grain the market had to bid what the government loan price was at least, so the farmer could make a living, although the farmer has always been satisfied with too little. I've been told by collectors, I've had a lot of contact with them too, that the farmer will put himself out and his family out, deprive himself and his family to pay his bills much more than people in the urban area. Now I don't think a farmer's a bit better in any respect than anybody else, but I have been told this by collecting agencies. They would say a farmer's wife would go without a dress where a person in the city, they wouldn't do this.

Do you think the Farmers' Holiday Movement fit into the times? That it just kind of reflected the spirit of the United States at this time?

I think so. We had actually, we had a young revolution down here. That's what Roosevelt said. He says, "We've got a revolution out there, haven't we?"

Well Milo Reno says, "I'm afraid we have."

And he says, "Well we've got to do something." And that's... they called it a governor's conference and had it in Sioux City, Iowa. And that time ever-normal grainary deal was brought out. Definitely the Holiday Association had a bearing on the legislation that was passed in Washington. It was through necessity. They couldn't have the farmer defying the law, and they threatened not to raise anything either. They didn't need to threaten them because most of them didn't have enough money to operate, unfortunately.

Did most of the people who were active in the Farmers' Holiday Movement support the Farmer-Labor Party?

I would say 90 percent of them.

You were active in that party?

I never held office, but I was always active in the party.

You campaigned?

I campaigned some. I always attended meetings and probably I've always been rather vocal sometimes at the expense of business. I can offend the Republicans at times and the people to the right. And I don't seem to learn!

You said that you knew Elmer Benson quite well?

I've known Elmer Benson since the early 30's.

How was he sympathetic towards the Farmers' Holiday?

Elmer Benson was very sympathetic towards the Farmers' Holiday. In fact one time the Holiday used to . . . the county officials used to have to go down and see Floyd Olson quite often. Elmer Benson was Commissioner of Banks and Banking under Floyd Olson. He told him one time, he says, "I might have to have the Holiday help me." He had a cabin on some farm and they were going to foreclose on that farm. And he says, "I may need them to help me out." We told him we'd be available. But I've known Elmer since the 30's and I've heard about him before. Very down-to-earth man; he'd just as soon talk to me as a millionaire. It don't make any difference to him if you got a nickel or a million dollars. It depends on what you are, actually.

I can remember during the Non-Partisan League days Ernie Lundeen, I think it was — I'm sure it was — was going to speak in Ortonville. And people'd come from way the north end of Big Stone County, that's thirty miles, that's plenty of driving in them days, to hear him. He didn't appear and he didn't appear. And John McGowan, who was for law and order, the sheriff of Swift County — of Big Stone County — and a few of the businessmen caught Ernie Lundeen, put him in a boxcar on the Soo [Line Railroad], and started him out. When the train started out they lost the boxcar and they were going to send him to Appleton, and here these all these people were waiting to hear Ernie Lundeen, who was running for U.S. Senate. And he was riding in a box car on the Soo locked up. Elmer Benson, I think, was eighteen years old. He got wind of it and he caught up with the train and when the train stopped in Appleton why he let him out and brought him over to the meeting. He didn't think that was cricket. Wasn't that cheap of them or anybody to do? And this was the sheriff who, a few years later, who was out to enforce the law. Now this wasn't legal either. I don't know where law and order was then. Wasn't very evident.

Did you work for Elmer Benson's election for governor?

I worked in the county, yes.

Do you remember the big kick-offs they used to have down in Appleton?

That's right. They had big bands, and oh they had big doings for Elmer. I don't think Elmer wanted this too much.

Wanted to be governor?

He wanted to be governor, but I mean he didn't want some of this display and some of this pomp. But you're more or less — you have to go along with the organization. In my mind the greatest governor we had was Elmer Benson. I'm not alone in this. People from other states think that. Fred Stover of the Associated Farmers of Iowa he said that Elmer was the greatest governor we ever had. I've heard him make that statement several times. Elmer would not compromise principles. The times Floyd Olson thought it was expedient to his career he would do it, but I don't want to underestimate Floyd Olson. He was one of our top governors. But with Elmer there was no compromise of principles; even if it cost him his office, he would not compromise.

He was for the farmer and the laborer.

He was for the farmer and laborer. Maybe it's kind of ironic he's a banker, and normally they're one of the . . . oh with Wall Street and the moneyed interests. But he can see that the masses of people would be better off with things that he worked for.

Was there anything specifically that Elmer Benson did for this region when he was governor? Or that the Farmer-Labor Party did for the area?

Not especially for this particular area. He was good for the state. One of the biggest deals he put across was when he called a special session of the Legislature to increase the iron ore tax from United States Steel and the other steel companies who were stealing iron. He said all we'd have left was a big hole up there and that's what we got now. Now they're polluting the lake. He was hated by the lumber interest. He helped the lumberjacks win a stike. He provided surplus commodities for them so they could eat and keep body and soul together, and they won the strike. And that didn't win him any favor with the big companies, big corporations. This was unheard of.

Lund, Guy
S529

Guy Lund was born in Diamond Lake Township in Lincoln County. After finishing school, he began farming in the same township where he was born. He was active in Farm Holiday and Farmers Union activities. Mr. Lund now resides in Pipestone, Minnesota.

Mr. Lund, could you tell us a little bit about your background, where you were born and a little bit about your parents maybe?

Well, I was born in Lincoln County in Diamond Lake Township; that's north of Lake Benton. Then I went to grade school (as far as I went is through the eighth grade), and then when I started farming, I started in the same township about two miles west of where my folks had lived. I started in 1932, and it was starting into the depression then. As time went on, it got worse and worse. I don't remember the exact date, but it must have been around 1936 or somewhere therein, that I joined the Farmers' Holiday Association.

Were you involved in some of the Holiday activities of stopping the produce from going to market?

To begin with I didn't belong to it . . . this holding back to see what the deal was. And they had stopped some sales before I ever joined. And after I joined we stopped a few foreclosures on farms at Ivanhoe. I never went to any of these other towns. Ivanhoe was the only one.

Just within the county then?

Ya. But a lot of the neighbors that had joined before I did went to different county seats and stopped mortgage foreclosures, and then not only on farm foreclosures, but they also stopped the sales on personal property foreclosures.

Where they would sell the livestock and the machinery and stuff?

Ya. That's when there was a sheriff's sale usually. The Farmers' Holiday would have certain bidders designated and they'd wear a red necktie and if anybody else bid, why they was just pushed off to a side and they would ignore their bids.

In other words, the Farm Holiday designated some person within their own group to be the bidders at the sale.

Right. Sometimes there might be a couple bidders or maybe three, four.

Did they bid against each other a little bit to make it a legal sale?

Well, I think they did at times bid a little bit against each other, but it was always in pennies. They'd start out at maybe 1 cent or a nickel or something like that, and when it was bid in and no further bids, well, then the auctioneer had to sell it. Well, then the intention was to buy these back as cheap as they could and then after the sale was over give it back to the farmer that owned it originally.

Was there any problem with giving it back to the farmer? Did the sheriff come back and clamp a lien on it again or....

I really didn't have anything to do in cases like that, but I had heard of cases where they tried to do something about it, but I don't know how far they got. Then when they started doing that, I heard too that when they bid in these cattle at a few cents, a lot of them hauled them away and then brought them back later on to try to avoid having the sheriff grab 'em again right away. So then he'd have to go to court and go through a lot more red tape to get 'em back.

Who usually held the mortgages for these farmers that lost their personal property? Was it the banks, mainly, or businessmen?

On personal property, it was usually the banks or there were a few cases of businessmen holding this.

Like the lumberyard or the elevator or something like that?

In the one case — I didn't get to go to this sale, because . . . it was even quite close to where I lived, but I was kind of under the weather that day and didn't get to go there — but in that case it was a doctor had the mortgage on this personal property, and as far as I know I think the man maybe owed him some rent too. But anyway, he was going to foreclose on this personal property. They had quite a rucus at that time, but I missed up on that one.

Did many people who were renting farms have to move, or did the landlord rather let them stay, do you remember?

I don't recall too much about the rent deals. Now there was a few cases where somebody would rent the land — that is the owner would rent it to another party — and we would stop that deal so that the original farmer could stay there.

How active was the Farm Holiday in Lincoln County? Do you feel it was a fairly active organization?

It was from the beginning, but it seemed to me like towards the last, when I got more active in it (at first I wasn't really active in it at all), but later on it seemed like some of the leadership just started going the opposite way and wasn't interested in helping the farmer. They even let the Farmers' Holiday drop to pieces. Well, then there was a small group of us took hold and kept it alive for another year or so.

Why do you think the leadership lost control?

I couldn't say for sure. It just seemed to be something political about their idea that at that time they had a few of these different political organizations starting up there were... well, I think a couple of the leaders even was in favor of Hitler's idea of change of government. And some of the... well, even the leaders in the Farmers Union went that way, too. Eventually, the Minnesota Farmers Union lost their charter and they had to start and reorganize all over again.

Because of the leadership being a little bit on the fascist side maybe or...?

Ya, and in order to keep control they wouldn't sign up new members that were opposed to them, and they had even kept records of people that had already died and considered them as members. So that was one way they could get rid of 'em, say that they were falsifying membership. I don't think they could have gotten rid of them on the political idea.

Why do you think these people went that way? Did they feel that was an answer to the farming problem, or were they doing it for their own personal gain?

It's hard to say just what the deal is, whether they didn't know any better or if they felt there would be some personal gain for themselves. Maybe they thought eventually there would be a change in government, and then they could be on top.

Do you think the leadership before this change was really concerned with the farmer and his welfare?

It seemed like they were.

They were sincerely committed to trying to better the farmer's lot?

Yes, I think they were.

Where did most of the Farm Holiday membership come from? What type of a background? Do you have any idea? I don't want you to say that 25 percent or anything like that, but generally in your opinion, where did the farmers that joined the Farm Holiday sort of fit in in the economic and political spectrum?

Well, they seemed like . . . it was all kinds of them that belonged to it. It just seemed it was their opinion that they do something about it. Sometimes they were real poor ones and sometimes they were pretty well, or at one time had been, better fixed farmers too that got in a pinch. Some of them were just as active in the Holiday as really poor ones.

Did you feel that there was any sort of a political thing that ran through there, that the more liberal type farmers belonged and the conservative ones stayed away?

I think what really happened was that before this change in the Farmers Union came, there was quite a few liberal people in there and instead of having the Farmers Union do all of this activity, they got together and organized this Farmers' Holiday Association so that the Holiday Association could have the brunt of the blame if anything bad happened. And in that case I would say that the Farmers Union members were mostly the ones that organized it. Of course, after it got going there were other ones that didn't belong to the Farmers Union that joined it, too.

Did these people who belonged to the Farmers Union and the Farm Holiday have dual membership in effect then?

Ya, a lot of them did have membership in both organizations. Then if someone would say it was a Farmers Union doing, well, no, Farmers Union doesn't do things like that, it's the Farmers' Holiday.

Oh. So the Holiday ended up being the scapegoat for the

GUY LUND

==Farmers Union and took the brunt of all the criticism.==

Ya, well that's to me how it was.

Did they have farm extension agents at that time in the thirties?

Oh yes, they did.

Where did they fit in on this picture? I know they were probably pretty much financed by Farm Bureau type organization.

Well, there was probably a lot of those that were really opposed to the Farmers' Holiday Association and then there was others that just didn't say much, they just let it go along the way . . . they didn't like to come right out and be opposed to some of these people who might be their own neighbors or own relatives.

Sort of the same type of thing we see today with the NFO maybe a little bit?

Ya, ya.

Did you get involved in any, or did you see any of the Farm Holiday activity, where they stopped the produce from going to market, where they blockaded the roads and things?

No, I wasn't in on any of that.

You weren't involved in any of that, then what did you think of that at the time, do you remember?

Well, in a way, I thought it would be a good thing if they could accomplish something, but to me it looked like they were going at it in the wrong way, because you'd hear that— now, I don't know if they started at first in Iowa, but they started down somewhere in the southern part and held produce off the market. Well, then by the time it got up to Minnesota and they were holding it off here, the ones down there were selling, so it seemed like a wave starting from the south and going north. So to me it looked like that way it was foolish, if they wasn't going to hold it all off at the same time.

You didn't think it was a very concerted effort?

No, I didn't think it was working out like they told about it should.

Do you think there was a lot of hoopla about it?

There seemed to be quite a bit of that, telling everybody, "You got to get in and help and get the prices back up."

Did they come around and see you at that time and ask you to join, or did they just sort of leave you alone?

Most generally they would leave you alone, because at that time I didn't belong to the Farmers Union. But I think they did perhaps go around and canvas members of the Farmers Union, but there was a neighbor of mine that got me to join. He had been in it maybe a year or two before I joined.

Why do you think the Farm Holiday died, other than that political problem you brought up? Why do you think the Farm Holiday didn't stay as an active organization?

Well you see, now I forget what year it was, but Benson was governor of Minnesota at that time, and he declared a moratorium that they couldn't have any more foreclosures in Minnesota. And from then on it seemed it died out quite fast.

It just sort of lost its need?

Ya, they didn't really need it to stop these foreclosures, and actually it was organized just as a temporary organization to take the pressure off the Farmers Union.

In other words, it wasn't really organized as a lasting organization?

No, I don't think it was ever intended to be a lasting organization.

How well organized do you think the organization was in Lincoln County? Was it very strongly organized or rather loosely organized?

I thought it was pretty strongly organized to begin with, but of course, you see, when there was something going on like stopping a foreclosure, people from other counties would come in to make sure there was enough strength. And on the start it seemed like they probably needed it, but later on, by the time I got active in there, even the sheriff was glad to have you stop the sale, or he could lose his, too.

Did you get involved with the . . . the Farm Holiday set up what they called arbitration committees within the townships and the counties to come up with some sort of equitable agreement between the mortgage holder and the farmer, to alleviate the possibility of stopping a foreclosure sale.

To begin with, I didn't have anything to do with that, although I did see where this . . . it was more like a self-appointed committee, that talked it over with the sheriff, what to do after they had stopped the sale, because he didn't want to have it sound like he was too willing to stop it. You know, he's got to do his job, too. So they would try to work out with him and make a date when they could meet with the people from these mortgage companies. Sometimes it was like Banker's Life Mortgage Company, Federal Land Bank or different companies like that. Then they'd get different representatives from them to meet with these representatives from the Farmers' Holiday Association to work out some kind of a deal. But later on, by the time it was beginning to die out and I was getting more towards the top of the Farmers' Holiday, I was on ... it actually wasn't a committee at all. It was just me and a couple other fellows that took it on ourselves to make an agreement.

Did some of the farmers that had mortgages with the insurance companies make a deal that they became renters for a period of time by giving the farm back to the insurance company? They stayed on the farm and they were no longer owners; they were then renters and rented it for a number of years from the insurance company?

I don't remember just what happened with those that were actually foreclosed on, if there was any kind of a deal like that. But we made a deal with those when we had stopped a sale that they were paying just like they were renting, until times could get better, so they could catch up and make up on their back payments. You see, these deals we set up, where they'd pay a third of their crop or two-fifths or whatever it happened to be, was never enough to cover the payments. It was always going backwards. It wasn't covering, so after the times got better then they could make up the difference that they lost. And I think a big share of them did, 'cause I know of different ones that kept their farms and got them paid for.

Did you live closer to Tyler or Lake Benton?

I was north of Lake Benton, a little bit west, most north.

What was the reaction in Lake Benton to this bunch of wild-eyed farmers running around the countryside, the businessmen downtown?

I don't think that I heard too much reaction against it, except when it would be one that had the mortgage. Then, of course, he was actually opposed to it. But otherwise a lot of them actually felt sorry for the farmers, and they needed their help in their business.

It was sort of "I'll help you, you help me" kind of thing.

Ya.

Did the women ever get involved in the Holiday in Lincoln County?

Not that I know of. They probably did in other places that I've read about, but I don't recall any in the country that really got involved to take action like they did in some places .... Did you get any report on the foreclosure at Milbank, South Dakota?

No, I haven't heard about that one.

That turned out to be kind of a rough deal.

Tell us about it.

Now, I wasn't there, but I got this information from the ones that were there.

Okay, that's just as good.

The sheriff out there — I don't even know what direction this farmer lived from Milbank, but it was out in that neighborhood — the sheriff had heard that they were going to stop the sale, so he got 180 deputies deputized. The farm place was back from the road aways, and so just the machinery was all lined up in a row between the road and the buildings. So he had his deputies stationed in there to protect the auctioneer and the banker that was taking care of the books. There was oh, perhaps, something like 3-4,000 farmers, and they'd park their cars down along the road, and of course a lot of 'em come in trucks. They'd load up a whole truckload and haul 'em there and then they'd start marching up there. Well, then these deputies were all lined up there to prevent them from coming any further than so far, so then if they was going to do any bidding they'd have to do it from outside the line. And each deputy had a revolver in his left hand and a billy club in his right hand, and they stood side by side with just enough room so they could work there. Some farmers got up pretty close, and one deputy must have gotten pretty excited an pulled a trigger on his revolver. One farmer hollered, "I'm shot," and the whole works of farmers, they just went over to the machinery. They didn't even stop to go around; they went over there and disarmed them 180 deputies. This man who was telling about it, he said, "I grabbed a wrist, one wrist of that man with a revolver in one hand and with a billy club in the other," and he said, everybody put 'em up just like that. And the rest of them never fired a shot. He says they probably never intended to, but this one must have accidentally pulled the trigger. And then they found out afterwards this fellow wasn't really hit at all. The bullet just come by his pant leg and he thought it hit him.

It could have very easily hit him.

It could have been....

Do you think there was a point where they were awfully close to an armed uprising in a situation like that, if something would have happened, if somebody would have gotten shot?

Well, if somebody had gotten shot there, I think it would have been pretty rough, because they'd have probably just beat 'em up, regardless if some more of 'em would have got shot. So it's hard to tell what would have happened.

It's hard to say any time what would have happened.

But you know, they would get pretty angry and do things they was sorry about afterwards too.

GUY LUND

The people got pretty emotional then, didn't they?

I think they did, especially if something like that happened. Otherwise a lot of times they just come up there and stood around like they was lookin' on to see what was goin' on. But I was at one foreclosure at Ivanhoe when there was only a small group there. That was when the Holiday was beginning to die out, and I think there was maybe 20-22 farmers there and when the sheriff started reading off his stuff, we just walked up and told him we wanted the sale stopped. And he says, "Well, come over to the office, I'll call up the mortgage company and see what kind of arrangements we can make." So he called them, and they evidently had asked him how many people was there and he says, "Oh, there's about 3,000 people here!"

How many people were there really?

Somewhere around 20 or maybe 22 or something like that! Of course he wanted to take the pressure off of himself, so he wanted to know what we should do. They says, "We'll meet with the representatives of the Farmers' Holiday Association and see what the wolves want to do." Well, I was one of 'em that met with them that time, and this farmer that we stopped the sale on, he was quite an old man. So he couldn't even read or write. If he wanted to sign his name he'd make an X. So we made a settlement and then he was supposed to pay 1/3 of his crop, and he was one of them that saved his farm that caught up on all his back payments later on. So it looked like at the time, a lot of these mortgage companies were trying to grab land cheap.

But yet you talk to some of the insurance companies and people who represented them, they said those companies didn't want the land.

Well, they talked like they didn't want it, but they sure were willing to take it!

Did you have to do some hard bargaining at those meetings when you tried to make a settlement of some kind?

Not at the time when I was one of them in this, what they called a committee. Most of them were getting used to it by that time, but I think on the start it was a little rough.

There was some pretty hard knocking heads together and bargaining type things?

See, I didn't get to any of those in the beginning, so I don't really know except what I'd heard that sometimes it was a little rough to make settlements.

But you never really had any problem. It was just sitting down and working an agreement out?

You'd just meet with them and say, "Well this farmer is willing to pay a share of his crop. He isn't trying to beat you out of anything."

Well, they'd say, "We're willing to accept any reasonable deal if he'll stick to it and not just sign something and say later on that he ain't gonna pay."

And we'd say, "We aren't there to try and skin you, we're there to see that the farmer does his part too so he can keep his farm."

Do you think there were farmers who were trying to get a free ride?

Oh, ya, there was a few. There was always a few, and it was hard to distinguish from people that come in, outsiders, who was the honest ones and who was the crooked ones.

Do you think basically they were pretty much all honest?

GUY LUND

I think the biggest share of them were honest then and now too. Usually if they get into a pinch, it isn't that they want to beat a person, it's just that they have a hard time paying.

What happened to all of the Farm Holiday people after the Farm Holiday died? Where did they all go? Did they go back to the Farmers Union, or did they just kind of drop out of all farm organizations?

Well, those that orginally were in the Farmers Union, see, they belonged to both organizations anyway, so they just dropped their membership in this Farmers' Holiday. Those that didn't belong to maybe any organization, well they just dropped it too and just left it the way it was. But by that time, it was beginning to get a little better times, and then pretty soon we got into the war and then things picked up a little more.

Do you think the war saved the farmers?

It probably did on prices, but I don't know about otherwise.

Some people have said that the Farm Holiday became, was able to rise up in Minnesota like it did because many of the farmers had the old Non-Partisan League background. Do you think that is true or . . . ?

I think it probably would make some difference, but you see, a lot of that see was before my time, that is before I was farming. I heard a lot about it when I was younger and before I started farming for myself.

Your father, would he have been involved in the Non-Partisan League?

No, he never. . .

He wouldn't touch it with a ten-foot pole!

Well, he wasn't just real against it, but my folks belonged to the Farm Bureau. But my dad wasn't really opposed to some of these organizations, if he thought they would eventually maybe do some good. But he says the Farmers' Holiday saved his farm and he never belonged to it.

Now he farmed during this period too, right?

Ya, he was farming. He had a quarter section of land, and at the time that the loan was supposed to be renewed he owed $2,000 on it. At that time things was pretty fair — see that was 10 years before this Holiday deal — and so he had the mortgage set so he had the mortgage at $2,000 on 80 acres and the other 80 acres with the building on was clear. Well then, that was a 10-year loan. Then that came due during the Farmers' Holiday deal, in the hard times in the thirties and the loan company wouldn't renew his loan, and they wouldn't renew it even if he put the $2,000 on the whole quarter, or if he had another section of land they wouldn't renew it. He says, "We're not renewing loans." So that looked like they were trying to take advantage. . . .

It looked like they wanted the farm.

Ya, just like they wanted it, but they would say, "Well, we don't want the land." Well I think they wanted land like that, but maybe they didn't want the ones that had a big mortgage on them.

They wanted one that they would make a lot of money on the long run.

So about the time that that was coming due was when this Farmers' Holiday activity was on, and they never got around to foreclose on him. Then in a short time they put on this moratorium, and then that saved him. Well in a few years, why he was able to pay his off. But he said if it hadn't been for the Farmers' Holiday Association, he evidently would have lost his. Well, he'd have lost that 80 acres that had that $2,000 on. He wouldn't lose the other because that was clear, unless something would happen that he'd get into debt so far that he'd have to hand them that to pay for it.

Farmers' Holiday Association protesters, Lac Qui Parle County, 1933. Donated by Oscar Torstenson.

Kelly, J. J.
S443

Mr. Kelly graduated from veterinary school in 1917, and he then served in WWI. After the War, he set up practice in Marshall from 1919-1960. He served as state legislator from 1956 until 1962.

Let me ask you Mr. Kelly, if you could recall a little bit about the Farm Holiday?

I recall it very vividly, the Farm Holiday Movement. A lot of my friends, people that were my good customers . . . I'm not here to say whether it was right or wrong, who am I to judge right or wrong on anything? But people were having a hard time getting enough to eat, and you know when people are hungry, they'll resort to a lot of things. And they saw their farms being moved away from them, being foreclosed. I happened to be handed a herd of cattle on test for a public auction and when I came out to make the reading the yard was full of cars and people in there. And one fellow, who was a very good friend of mine, came over and he said, "Doc, I wouldn't bother going to the trouble of reading those cattle," he said, "there's not going to be any sale."

And I said, "Well, that's OK with me. The only thing is," I said, "if I've already tested them, I should read them, because maybe there will be a sale later on and then the farmer won't have to go to the trouble of having them retested."

"Well," he said, "whatever you think is all right."

So, we didn't; they didn't have the sale.

And then on this Farm Holiday, I was going out on a call out on north 59 and they were congregating to come in, march into Marshall that afternoon, which they did. They marched in and what opposition they got, they overpowered the opposition. There were so many of them. In fact, they took the sheriff's gun away from him and made him stand there while they talked this thing over, mapped their strategy. And then Senator Regnier, at that time he got up and made an impassionate plea to arbitrate the thing, send the committee or name a committee to go in and talk it over with the powers. So they went in and talked it over at Swifts, and the manager agreed to close down and then they all marched down, 10 or 12 abreast, on Main Street singing and hollering. They had scored a victory.

But that was the end of the Holiday Association. There wasn't any more Holiday. I think that the governor, who at that time was Floyd Olson . . . by the way, a good friend of mine; he was a Farmer-Laborite and I was a strict Democrat. I didn't even go for the Farmer-Laborite. He called them off. He told them they'd have to quit that. There was going to be a demand by the people that they call out the National Guard, and that's one thing that he didn't want to do. That's suicide for any governor to do. That was really the end of it. Oh, they had meetings, sure, but that was the last demonstration. I think Swifts started up in about a week. There was nothing done about it, and they just started up and there was nothing done after that.

What accomplishments did the farmers get from the demonstrations?

I don't really think they got too much, except to show that they could be united a little bit when they had to be and that they were. They had a just cause. They weren't getting anything. In fact, corn was 10¢ and cattle about 3¢; 10¢ corn and 3¢ steers. I can still hear Senator Kerr's keynote speech when he talked about 10¢ corn and 3¢ steers.

Can't make any money that way.

No, you couldn't even pay...

Were the farmers having trouble getting credit to carry them through these times?

They couldn't get credit. There was no credit.

There was no credit.

There was no money to lend. Let's see, that was in, when was that did I say?

'33, probably?

It was along in that time, but I know you couldn't borrow money at the banks. In fact, the banks had been closed up and reopened.

Bank Holiday.

The Bank Holiday, yes. That's how come my wife said we're never going to be without money again. In fact, I went to the bank the day before they closed them up. I had probably 75, 80 dollars in checks and cash. I put them in the bank. That was a lot of money; that was more money than you see anytime. It focused attention on the condition of the farmers, and they were in bad shape.

This gave them a lot of visibility then.

From then on, you know, they did a lot of things. They had the PWA and CWA, work programs. We all know they didn't do much good for the country, but they got some money into circulation and we got something to eat and from there on we started cutting back.

Do you see any connection between the Farm Holiday demonstrations and the passage of the mortgage moratorium laws for the farmers?

Oh, you mean, when they, you mean moratorium where they couldn't...

Foreclose.

Foreclose. Well, I think that was as a result of the Holiday Association's demonstrations. They found out they had to do something. They couldn't let these people starve.

How many... I don't want any numbers, but from your experience did you see a lot of fellows lose farms in the twenties and thirties?

Oh, just pitiful. Men who had farmed all their lives. I know a lot of them. Of course, there's one thing I will say, and I'll always give the insurance credit. I think they were fair. Anybody that's lost their farm or was foreclosed, they gave them a chance to buy it back. They didn't sell it away from them. And they could have hung on to this. Of course, the laws in the United States said they had to get these farms off their books, they couldn't carry them as an asset anymore. They had to get rid of them. So they sold them, gave them very good terms. I know a lot of people that are rich that bought those farms, today.

Most of the farm mortgages were held by insurance companies?

They were all held by insurance companies. Most of the farms that were held by the insurance companies were in turn turned over to the trust companies. They were held in trust for the insurance companies. That's what they had to do. I had a nephew that worked for Northwest Mortgage & Trust, and he was out in Montana, and he said you find any ranch you want, I'll get it for you, for little or nothing. You can sell this land for a dollar an acre out there, a lot of it, and the insurance companies had to get it off their books. They, Northwest Mortgage & Trust, were holding a lot of these farms in trust for the insurance companies. Not only in Montana.

Do you feel the insurance companies, though, gave the farmer a good chance to buy the land?

I think they did. Yes, they did. They gave him a chance. And on very liberal terms, too. In fact, there were some people that got rich off it. Well, I can show you a lot of farmers around here that would be, wouldn't be here today if it weren't for the farm moratorium. They'd have lost their farms . . .

That saved a lot of farms, then, that moratorium?

Yes, it did. That was one of the good things that, in my estimation, was one of the good things that came out of the mill. I think it was pushed along a little bit by that Farm Holiday meeting. It had some impact on the country and I think they weren't all bad, by any means. There were some good things that they were responsible for. Not all of them, but they were responsible for getting attention.

These demonstrations in Marshall, would you estimate that a good proportion of these demonstrations were basically local people or were a large number . . .

Well, there were some of them. They say there were paid agitators in there, and communists, but I couldn't see any. I knew most of these people.

You saw a large number of local people?

I know darned well they were local, 'cause there were a lot of my friends in there.

They felt they needed some desperate action to . . .

That's right. They had to do something to jar this thing loose, and from then on why things started to loosen up. They had the PWA, and even if they only did get 10 or 12 dollars, that was 10 or 12 dollars more than they had the week before that. There was a nice part about that. You couldn't ... well, then we had other things, you know. They had this cattle-buying program where the cattle ... there was no feed. We hadn't had crops here, you know, for a long time. These cattle were starving. They initiated cattle and then the government started buying these drought cattle and I was on that from start to finish, buying those drought cattle.

The government would buy them at a ...

They had a set price for a certain class of cattle. It was 8, 12 and 20; 8, 12, 15 and 20. The big steer only weighed 1,000 pounds. You could only get 20 dollars for him, that was the most you could get. But there was a certain part of that. The check went direct to the grower. The bank couldn't touch it.

So this was government relief for the drought ...

It was a cattle reduction program in the way they bought these cattle, slaughtered them, and put it in. And then they sent that back here in bacon and, oh, stuff like that. And then they took a lot of these cattle, which was a very foolish thing to do. I don't know who was ... well a good friend, Goody Sonstegard, was the guy that was in charge of it out in this country. When the man would bring his cattle in to sell, they'd pick out the likely well-bred cattle for foundation and kept them for foundation, or they sent them up to ... I can't think of that place right north of Minneapolis there, or north of St. Paul. I don't have much of a memory anymore of times and places. But anyhow, they sent them up there and branded them and tagged them and they took them up and turned them loose in the Superior National Forest. They haven't seen them since.

What was the purpose of turning them loose in the forest?

Well, there was food up there. And they turned them loose. They were going to bring them back in. Well, the Indians killed most of them. They called them slow deer.

Did they honestly expect to graze them up there?

They did graze them.

That was their purpose?

Sure. That's why they sent them up there, but they figured they'd get them back again. They branded them and tagged them. That doesn't mean anything to the Indians. They can't read anyhow.

Photo courtesy S.S.U. Southwest Minnesota Historical Center.

Goede, William C.
S429

Mr. Goede has been a farmer all of his life. He also served as town clerk and school clerk. He was active in the Democratic Farmer/Labor party. Mr. Goede was secretary of the Jackson County Farm Holiday Association.

To start off the interview, Mr. Goede, I think we will ask you a little bit about your background, where you were born and what line of work you have been in most of your life.

Well, I have been a farmer all my life. I had been town clerk here for fifteen years and a school clerk for 25 years. One time I was secretary to three organizations and it about drove me nuts. I was quite active in the DFL, but now I found so many crooks in there, just as in the other party, that we quit it entirely. I was committee clerk in 1937 in the state legislature. I was a Farm Laborite at the time, see, but they were out. The Republicans took ahold of the thing for a number of years; they appointed their friends. In 1957, that's when I quit farming and went on Social Security.

How did you get involved in the Farm Holiday?

I was sitting in the audience in Lakefield and it so happened that Hemming Nelson, a state representative, spied me in the audience, and he is the one that made the motion. That's the biggest mistake I ever made, because a man raising a family should stay home once in a while. I was on the road more than I was at home. The principle involved is still there yet. He pointed me out in the audience there in Lakefield. He was vice chairman of the Farmers Union and it was the Farmers Union that sponsored the organization of the Farm Holiday here. The same as any other farm organization, they started telling you they are going to get better prices. My reason for involvement is the fact that I believed in the cost of production, which covered expenses, but there again, the federal government has taken ahold of things in pretty fair shape along that line. My favorite sermon was, we are engaged in an occupation where we produce a commodity that is essential to the very existence of banking, and yet we have no voice in the determination of the value, not at all. But we are coming. I am afraid there are certain elements that go a little too far. I don't believe in violence, you don't get anywhere with that.

This meeting that Mr. Nelson was to speak at, was that an organization meeting, to organize the Farm Holiday?

It was a Farm Union meeting for the purpose of organizing the Farm Holiday and he knew me because I had been up in the legislature as a clerk and I knew who he was. We believed the farmer had something to say about the value of his farm products.

In other words, you are saying that the Farmers Union had a meeting to organize the Farm Holiday?

They did that; in fact Hemming Nelson was the vice chairman of the Farm Union of this state at that time.

Was John Bosch down here for that?

I remember him too, ya. I remember when I was up in the legislature, I heard him tell this himself; he had some lady secretary there, and of course the custom around there was the men would take them out to lunch. He found out they could drink more beer than he could.

You were elected the secretary of the Farm Holiday, weren't you?

Yes, and I never kept any minutes and anything that I tell you will have to be from memory. I did keep a financial record and about a month ago I decided that the financial book is at the bottom of my trunk. It would take me a half a day to get. So we believed as they believe in all organizations, of course. The Farm Bureau and the Union are getting together much better now than they used to be. They were so far apart there wasn't any resemblance of the same policy. They had been busted long enough, some of them, that they finally woke up. If you run a store and I come in there and wanted bananas and I told you I will give you a dime for a hundred bananas, you would have to take it if you were a farmer. That is the way the thing is run.

When you organized the Farm Holiday, you set up on a township level, right?

Well, I would say so more or less.

You were involved in the county-wide organization?

Well, I was yes. We had a pretty fair organization here for a while. We put on a strike here once; that was something that was new. My wife was at a ladies aid meeting and they said those farmers are getting rambunctious here dumping out the cream and the eggs and stuff. That was so in some localities, but not here. So I called up the city clerk and I told him what the rumor was and that there was nothing to it. I said this is a battle between the agricultural west and the industrial east. If anyone is in need of stuff, we will establish a food depot at the armory, give them the cream and eggs and not charge them a nickel. We want them on our side. So it was to get some recognition for the fact that the farmer is entitled to a voice in determining the value of his product. Well, it simply woke them up a little bit.

Francis Shoemaker was a congressman and he had called up Washington and told them they were drilling here, the big liar, so as not to get caught technically. Why the national guard was drilling in every county seat—they were drilling, not for anything offensive.

When you had your strike, around Jackson here, did you keep the produce from going to Jackson?

Ya, we had a strike for four days and then we lifted it. But the farmers didn't remain loyal. People on the north side of this county were taking their stuff to Windom, the west side would take to Worthington, the east side would take to Spirit Lake, so we just forgot it. They just were not ready for anything like that.

It wasn't successful then?

No, it didn't accomplish anything. There was some violence in different areas, according to the newspapers.

There wasn't any trouble here? Did anybody try to run your blockade, to break through the blockade you had set up?

No, I don't think so, they just begged us to quit, that is about all. We saw what was happening, that unless this was done all over in a county like Jackson or any other county it wouldn't help any. It had to be nation-wide.

Did you put up a blockade around Lakefield?

No, we didn't; just Jackson.

Were there quite a few farmers out there on the blockade? Out on the road with you to stop trucks?

Well, I just don't remember exactly. They did up toward Windom, at Bergen, about 11 miles north of here. They stopped Ashley [?], but he was smarter than they were. He had them in for supper and while they were in for supper, the trucks pulled out with a load of cattle. But it was the beginning of a new idea which finally developed to what we have today. The federal government knows enough about agriculture now that we are safe if they could just get to the point where the

WILLIAM GOEDE

Farm Bureau and the Farmers Union and the Minnesota Cooperatives and various other organizations had a voice in determining a price. How do I know what I am going to get? We have an 80 acre farm here and my nephew is farming his father's place across the road, the 80 here and the 40 he bought, how do we know at the present time, what will we get for the 400 bushels of beans we have stored here?

Do you think a lot of the farmers in this township belonged the Farm Holiday?

Well, I remember that 30 of them were of the Non-Partisan League, part of them were Republican, and part of them were Democrats. I couldn't say as to how many, but there was quite a number that did, because it was the Union that helped organize it.

How many of the farmers belonged to the Farmers Union? A majority of them?

Well, there was 30 of them right here in this locality. Because these leaders of the Bohemians led it, and they would follow them and a couple of more would naturally take their word for whatever they represented.

After your strike failed, you started helping people losing their farms, these foreclosures sales?

That's where we did some good. I sat at many a meeting. I didn't believe in this rough stuff. It was on a Friday night, we were in Lakefield, it was snowing and Charley Johnson was the chairman at the time and I was secretary. A fellow from Wilder and his son appealed to us to help him settle his mortgage on his personal property; the insurance company was going to foreclose on Tuesday. So I told Charley, "You had better come along with me." We met in back end of Nicholas' office. They were going into court at 2:00 in the afternoon and there was a fine appearing young man that represented the insurance company from Spencer. Now I said, "I am going to hold the chair today. Don't get the idea that I got a crowd here because we're gonna lick you, we're not going to do anything I can't do myself." I said, "You are the one that has got the money coming, what do you want? Get that first, then I will tell what we will do. What do you want so this man can keep his personal property and the sheriff does not take it to the fairgrounds? What do you want us to do?"

He said, "If you can raise three hundred dollars so that you can buy your hay and your corn and stuff back and stay right where you are." He got the three hundred. This man said, well if they raise so much money—I think it was three hundred, I am not sure—but to raise enough money to buy this stuff back, how much do you want for the hay, how much do you want for so many bushels of corn, how many oats and he gave the straw. He was very nice to deal with.

So when we got through, had all the stuff bought back, there was one stack of corn fodder left. This one fellow, who was broke, had no more money but he was depending on relatives for groceries and help for a while until he got on his feet again. "Well," he said, "I will tell you, in my own mind I thought that fodder was worth fifteen dollars," but this young man said, "I will tell you, I have never dealt with a better bunch than I have here this afternoon and to show my appreciation I will do what is right about that fodder, you give me five dollars for that fodder and you can have it." I wrote a check on the organization, which I had the authority to do, and give this insurance man the five dollars and low and behold, when I first went up there and asked, I met the sheriff down below and said, "Chris, you don't have to put that stuff in the fairgrounds Tuesday."

He put his arms around me, and said, "I hated to do it, but I had to do it." I told him about the five dollars. He had a heart and he reached in his pocket and took out his checkbook and reimbursed the five dollars. And that settled that.

Another time in Lakefield, a fellow by the name of Billy Craft had some trouble with his farm mortgage and the chairman wasn't there, so I held the chair. I asked him the same question. I told the insurance man, "Now you state what you want. You got the money coming. What do you really want?"

Billy Craft started butting in, and I said, "Now you keep still, This is where we take one thing at a time. You can't mix it all up here. You wait until this insurance man gets through and then you can state your position." Well, it came to pass, he went to the bank and borrowed the money to pay this insurance man. He was able to borrow 300 dollars with that whole crowd—there were 6 of us there—couldn't have borrowed 300 dollars and neither could have I. So, he borrowed 300 dollars and paid the insurance man and that settled that. That's the way you settle those things, many of them.

Here is what happened; Farmers Union started to organize the Farm Holiday and then Governor Olson set up a committee of seven men to handle this. The federal government took it over and handled it nationally and three—a banker in Heron Lake, myself, and I forgot who the other fellow was on the committee. The demand was so bad that I finally brought a man here that worked for nothing, kept his board and room to do my chores. "I resign," I said; "I can't take this. I got small children and I got to get home part of the time. We did not get any pay; they offered us once in a while, but nothing doing. Then finally prices began to come up better and everybody forgot the Farm Holiday. They did not forget the Farmers Union and they never will. They can't lick the Farmers Union, they might as well make up their minds to that.

Did you ever go to the courthouses and stop a mortgage sale?

I tell you, we were at, I think it was near Fairmont one time, a big crowd gathered there at a farm place and I just don't remember. A state representative helped settle that, whatever it was. There was a demonstration once, but I wasn't there.

You never stopped any sheriff sales at the courthouse then?

Not there, but they did at other sales. One of the tricks they used, I heard about, when the sheriff went to read the paper someone would put their hand over the top of the paper and shake hands with him and the sheriff couldn't read the proceedings. They stopped quite a few sales and then they quit. That's when Governor Olson appointed seven men to help settle, then the federal government. What really solved the problem was this: the federal government organized the farm credit organization and they subsidized the Federal Land Banks and wherever a man had a foreclosure, why we made applications for a Federal Land Bank loan. The insurance company had to have their money. They couldn't go out any more, they were so far gone. So that is the way they settled it—by organizing the National Farm Credit Administration which subsidized Federal Land Bank, and that solved the problem right there. But the beginning was a big noise. I was threatened with a foreclosure myself here on this eighty. I had nine thousand dollars debt on his eighty at one time. I bought it for fifty-five hundred, after setting up household, raising a family, and my wife was sick quite a bit. The Federal Land Bank solved the problem for the farmers; the Farm Credit Administration solved the problem. It started somewhere and finally got to a point where there was some horse sense.

Were there any penny sales in Jackson County?

Well, there were some foreclosures. The Farm Holiday lasted just until Governor Olson appointed that committee and that wiped out the Farm Holiday right then and there. See, the Farm Holiday was farm-sponsored and the committees were government-sponsored, there was more to it.

Did you go around and help organize the Farm Holiday? Did you go around and visit the farmers and see if they would sign up for the Farm Holiday in your township?

Well, yes. I did some of that. What I really did was go out and appoint someone to take care of his township and do it themselves. If they wanted it, all right; if they didn't, that was it. Everybody was so hard up and broke that it wasn't a hard proposition.

Did most of the townships have quite a few people that joined then?

Well, I can't say offhand, but this township had quite a few. Where it was most active was up in Kimball Township. So I couldn't say offhand; that was quite a while ago. Generally where there was no leader what we would do was pick a leader, a man that was on the school board or the town board. If he didn't perculate, we fired him and got a different one.

Photo courtesy S.S.U. Southwest Minnesota Historical Center.

Farmers' Holiday protest at Swifts & Co., Marshall, Minnesota, November 10, 1933.

Runholt, Vernon
S188

Mr. Runholt is a farmer who has been living in the Marshall, Minnesota area since 1941. He grew up and attended school in Cottonwood, Minnesota and went to Bethany Lutheran College in Mankato for 1 year.

We got past the 30's before we asked them if they did have any reflection on the Farm Holiday Association. Since you did have one remarkable letter in your possession that did give some description of that, what is your own recollections or feelings about that period?

Well...I compared it to the period that's just past. Many of these people that were in the Farm Holiday movement were young people at that time... many, many lawless acts can be credited to the Farm Holiday, there's no question about that. For instance, one of our upstanding neighbors was one of the fellows with a baseball bat, beating the sheriff's car down here in Marshall. Most of the incidents at Marshall were by imported farmers—most of them were not Lyon County farmers—that came from farther north.

About how many were there? Do you have any idea?

I don't have any idea, but I think there was somewhere between 500 and 1000 farmers.

Do you think there was any benefit, in total, from the Farm Holiday, aside from these separate acts?

It tended to focus the attention of the country on the problem that the rural area was going through at the time. It has an effect in that the farm program of the 30's was probably boosted along a little more by what took place.

Do you think that Governor Olson helped a lot in that period?

He certainly did.

So you see it totally as a helpful thing in terms of focusing attention on the farm pride, therefore making it easier to get decent farm policies?

I think I'd have to say that I'm certainly not an advocate of what took place in these years or what took place then, but it did have this effect.

Nystrom, William
S194

Mr. Nystrom was born on the farm place where he now lives. He served as county president and Minnesota vice president of the Farmers Union.

How can you assess the emotional attitude of the farmers in 1932-33? Some people have maintained that the farmers were close to rebellion in 1932-33. How do you react to that? Do you think that's an accurate statement?

Well, in some areas that was true. They did get going a Farm Holiday Association. I know I did attend one farm sale down at Allendorf, Iowa, which is across the line from here. We heard the sale was coming so we went. It was a sheriff's sale. The sale started off . . . of course there was some bidders there that were going to bid the prices up, but the farmers there got them out of the way and what have you, and so the farm sale was never held. Now there was a good many farmers who owed bills here and there and so on. I did get on one committee there at one time, and there were three on the committee here in Nobles County, to try to scale down some of the debts the farmers owed to the others in business in town. They just didn't have the money to pay. We met with the two parties concerned and tried to compromise a little where a settlement could be made between the two parties. It did work successful to a large extent, and a lot of bills were scaled down that way. I'll give credit to a lot of business firms . . . that they were willing to do that.

Now getting back to those times of the Depression. When we went to Washington in the spring of '33 to lobby for farm legislation. . . well, we went down, we rode in a Model A

Ford. Roads weren't what they are now and it took more time; there wasn't motels along the line. We stayed at private homes; they had the shingles out and they were looking for people coming through to stay overnight and they'd pick up a dollar here and there.

Now the problem was, as far as farmers were concerned in going to Washington at that time it still would cost money to go, and farmers didn't have any money, and as far as farm organizations, some well, they didn't have money to go with either, so we went out to solicit funds. So two of us here, one fellow by the name of Louis Ross—lived just north of Worthington, and he was a couple, three years younger than I was—we went into Worthington, and the first fellow we wanted to see was I. O. Olson. He had a creamery there in Worthington, and produce and what have you, and he was a public-spirited fellow and was willing to help on every occasion. We explained to him where we were going and what we were going to try to do, and we were looking for some financial help. Mr. Olson, he gave us $25. We started the list there on donations and he was the first one; he put down $25. But he told us, he says, "Something has to be done. Go and see the other fellows on Main Street and see what they'll do. If you don't happen to get enough money to go, come back and I'll give you more."

Now this is some history I haven't told around very much, but the next person we went and saw was Mr. Habbick. He had a dry goods store, quite a large one and what have you. We explained to him what we were trying to do. Yes, he said, he'd be willing to donate. Well, he gave us a little advice. "The Chamber of Commerce Association, they've got rules laid down. If any member of this association donates to any cause that hasn't been approved by the committee of this Chamber of Commerce, they would be subject to fine." So we went and saw the secretary of the Chamber of Commerce, and he said he'd get his committee together. So we suggested that we might be able to meet with the committee, for there might be questions they'd like to ask and some things we'd like to tell them. But he said this was a secret committee. So we couldn't appear with the committee. We hung around and waited out in the street there for, I suppose, a half an hour or so, and here the **secretary** came back and said that we were turned down; they wouldn't approve our solicitation.

Now you want to remember that Mr. Habbick told us that they were subject to fine if they donated without the approval of this committee on any solicitation. But when we went back to Mr. Habbick and we told him that we had been turned down he said, "Give me the pencil." And he wrote down $10. Now $10 don't sound very much now, and it isn't, it'd be just a drop in the bucket. But $10 then meant something. From there on we went and saw all the business places there along Main Street, and even went up on the second floor where there were insurance and lawyer offices and went down to the courthouse and what have you. We got enough donations there in sending one to Washington D.C. Anyway, it so happened that the board picked me out for the one to go for Nobles County. When I came back I appeared one evening before the Chamber of Commerce meeting and told them about what we did in Washington, and what we tried to accomplish, and what have you. That also took place from other counties here in Minnesota which were organized at that time, and also the other states where we had Farmers Union organized. The Congressmen, they listened, and I think we did quite an effective work.

Was the union pretty well organized here in Nobles County? Do you have any idea of your strength, the percentage of farmers you had in the organization?

Yes, we're pretty well organized. There at one time, about in 1952 or somewhere in there, then we had gone up to 1400 members here in Nobles County in the Farmers Union. We had organizations in some townships prior to that, and then we went into these other townships that were unorganized. Of course there's considerable less farmers now in Nobles

County now than at that time. We had approximately around 700 at this time. I do repeat here again that as far as our membership, is strictly farm membership.

Was there any connection between the Farmers Union and the Farm Holiday?

Yes, there was . . . they were two different organizations entirely. But in a lot of areas, I will say Farmers Union members were a good many times instrumental in getting the Farm Holiday Association organized. There was one way as far as bringing the protest, the attention to the low farm prices and what was going on in agriculture to the rest of the nation. And it had its effect. Well, sure . . . I don't care what strikes or whatever picketing you do, sometimes it can get a little bit rough, there's no getting around that. But there wasn't too much of that happened here in Nobles County, but in some areas there was. Certainly when times get tough and you don't know where to turn to get your next dollar and you got bills to pay and you got a family to feed and what have you and you didn't get enough for your farm products to pay your taxes, why, some nice people will get a little bit desperate and most anybody will in a case like that. What are you going to do? What are you going to reach for? What's going to happen? What are we going to do about it? That's a problem too and the farm situation is the same today, too—just which is the best method to take, and what should we do? There's a lot of different opinions on it. Well, them days is the same as now. Farmers, they're a little bit harder to organize; they live individually out on each farm. They have different opinions and what have you. But, I will give credit to organizations that you do have in your towns, the various business groups and professional groups. Now, I had the experience of serving in the legislature a couple of terms, and, well, surprising, and that was back in '35 and '37, and being a farmer was all I had and always will be, I guess. But you find as a rule farmers don't take too much interest. During the times of legislature I don't suppose in two terms I got over a half dozen letters from farmers. But these other organized groups in business and what have you, I heard from them all. They done an effective job as far as lobbying is concerned. Well, in most cases they got their legislation passed.

The farmers weren't as well organized, then, in '35 and '37 as the business groups or other profesional groups? Farmers weren't effective in lobbying?

No, that is right. Farmers, they were kind of used to raising their crops and doing the best job they can and take whatever price was offered. Well, you know, as far as farmers are concerned, when we go and buy, the price is set. Either you take it or leave it. But when you haul your grain into market—and livestock, too—well, there's what they call the market price. There's where it is so important on farm program and support prices. At least there is a floor level there, where you can take a loan on your grain if you got storage out on your farm, or if you take storage in an elevator you can do that and if the market goes up you can always buy the grain back and in a good many cases you probably made a little profit on it.

In the thirties John Bosch was head of the Farm Holiday Association here in Minnesota. Did you have any dealings with him at all?

No, I didn't, although I did get acquainted with John Bosch and I know him well. He made meetings here in Nobles County. Certainly after the Depression kind of went by the wayside, of course, the Holiday Association also didn't function any more, and John Bosch did get into the Farmers Union and was active in support of the Farmers Union and at conventions and what have you. He was good to present his ideas on what he thought should be done. John Bosch, he did agriculture a valuable piece of work.

How do you think some people viewed Bosch? Was he viewed as kind of a dangerous radical by some people who weren't sympathetic to the Holiday, perhaps?

Well, of course, that is right. They would . . . you know, anything kind of new or something different than the way it's been going, or the way they have been doing it and so on, any change brought about, they want to call it radical. Well, you know, what was radical back there in those days, in the 30's, that isn't radical any more now. But, any change that takes place is considered by some as radical. Any change that is going to take place, it takes time.

How do you react to the comments that people make that they saw a communist influence in the Holiday Association? Did that ever trouble you at all? Did you think there was any foundation to that, any truth in that?

Well, you know, we heard a lot about that, communists and what have you. Well, even in the Farmers Union, commencing with the fifties, some of our opponents tore our organization. They wanted to call the Farmers Union communists in that, too, and the communistic leanings and so on. But we don't hear any more of that now, and, well, I have told you, at that time, a good many of them, that as far if you're going to be a member of the Farmers Union you have to be a farmer to be a member, and I think there are less communists among farmers than any other group. It's something the opposition used to try to scare people with. The opposition to the Farmers Union was really going out on an expansion program here in Minnesota; they wanted to use that on the Farmers Union, too. There was communists in it and the communistic influence. But the opposition, they did have [Herbert] Philbrick; you all remember him on T.V. They had him in Iowa, and I attended a meeting down in Iowa one time and he spoke there. I went and talked to Mr. Philbrick afterwards and told him where he was wrong, but he never made any statement to me or anything whatsoever. But Philbrick, he became a thing of the past. In the state of Idaho, the opposing farm organization at that time, this other Farmer's Union, had made statement that the Farmers Union were communistic and they were sued. Now they had made public statement, and they had it in black and white, and they had to pay some damages and retract what they said and whatever it was.

In Idaho you won a court suit?

Yeah, that is right. The same way there, too, in Congress. They had one senator there, the opposition to the Farmers Union; he wasn't from any agricultural state. He made a speech there in Congress attacking the Farmers Union and wanted to put them on communistic leaning and what have you. But as far as those that are in Congress, the same thing as far as those that are members of the legislature—it was true during the time that I was in the legislature—we had that protection that as far as whatever we stated, stated whether it was in Congress, Minnesota legislature, and so on, he was not held liable for it any place else except in the legislature. Nobody could sue you for your remarks. They used those things, but I mean as far as law suits, we beat them. You just don't hear of it any more at all. They weren't able to stop our organization, we continued growing and getting stronger and carried more influence. As far as the Farmers Union, it is a good respectable organization.

Do you consider yourself a radical, politically?

No, I don't. Sure, the Farmers Union. I also served as county president in another organization here. I have been on the State Board of Minnesota Farmers Union. And I've served 21 years... vice president of the Minnesota Farmers Union. And I retired last fall at our convention. I said I've been on now for 21 years, so now let someone younger take over and I thought I had done my bit. So I've served 21 years as vice president of the Minnesota Farmers Union.

What kinds of help did the Olson administration in Minnesota give to the farm movement?

Well, Olson . . . Minnesota at that time had three political parties—Republicans, Democrats, and got organized the Farmer Labor Party. There's where Floyd B. Olson ran for governor on the Farm Labor Party and he was elected. Now Governor Olson, he was quite a fellow; he had a lot of ability, he had a lot of following and he did what he could. There has to also be national legislation and national help, when there's really trouble and that's what is happening today on the welfare and everything else that you may say. Well, efforts were made: reducing interest rates and what have you, and postpone foreclosures and so on. That was one of the things that was accomplished. When farm prices were so low there was nothing to pay with, it certainly was wrong that those that they had borrowed money from, that they could foreclose on them. That was a valuable piece of legislation. There was a good many farms and a good many homes that were saved that way.

You see the postponing of foreclosures as a major contributon to the Olson administration?

Yes, yes, yes, it was . . . that's right . . . that was.

Meehl, Percy
S442

Percy Meehl was born in Lyon County on April 23, 1903. Mr. Meehl was a rural school teacher, an attorney (county attorney during the Depression), municipal judge, and United States magistrate. He practiced law in Marshall, Minnesota up until his death in 1981.

One of our special interests that we've been trying to gather information on is some of the farm activities of the 30's and the reaction of the farmers. What remembrances do you have of Farm Holiday?

Well, in Lyon County it wasn't bad, except in one instance. In general, though, these counties in western Minnesota we had lots of trouble when we'd go to foreclose a mortgage. They had an association known as the Farm Holiday Association and they would come in mobs to the foreclosure. In many instances the crowd around the sheriff would prevent him from reading the notice and just prevent him from making the sale. Of course, those sheriffs were quite sympathetic to the Holiday people because they voted also and they had to look out for votes. And in those days a public officer was just like a public officer today; the first thing he looks out for is votes and the next thing his job. But in Lyon County we had a couple of instances where they marched on this county and on the Swift plant. Swift was then manufacturing butter and sweet cream, where the turkey plant is up here now. I think Swift's have a turkey plant. They came in here about 2,000 that time.

When would this have been? '33 or '34?

About November of 1933 or 34. And they were quite bad. I know they tipped a fire truck over and assaulted the mayor and made very serious threats both on me and on the sheriff. I had some protection for two or three days, not that I . . . I guess it was more than that. They were very violent; they carried some plugs . . . .

Was this an organized effort or was it a spontaneous thing?

No, no, it was well organized. They had these associations in various counties, chapters of the Farm Holiday Association and they were genuine rebels, no question about it.

How did you and the sheriff handle this? How did you try and handle it? You just don't handle 2,000 people. What was your reaction to all this?

Just sent word out that we would be as calm about it as we could and we expected law enforcement and looked the other and just . . .

You try to be flexible.

Yes, just try to avoid any violence and try to avoid any damage.

Was there any violence or damage?

Oh, yes. There was damage and there was violence. There was lots of damage up here at the Swift plant and in many of the creameries; there was lots of violence, where they poured kerosene in the butter tubs. That was a common thing that they would do. And they tipped an automobile over and tipped a milk truck over and spilled the milk cans. And if a farmer tried to sell his cream in violation of what the Holiday Association, they'd pour the cream on the . . .

Was there any human violence?

Well, out here at Canby a man was shot; now that was a

striker. He was blocking the roads and someone came along and shot him. I know Murphy of Wheaton defended him. There were two or three people who lost their life one way or another.

But none in Marshall.

No, nobody in this area.

So it was just property damage.

Property here, yes. They damaged a fire truck here in town quite badly.

These people that marched in Marshall, were they basically local people?

Oh, they were from Granite Falls and Montevideo and organizations. Of course there were some local people. We had some of about the same stripe, more modern type since that time, that's the NFO, the National Farm Organization. That's a younger group of men more highly and better organized, of course. That's a good organization today, I think that NFO . . . .

Do you think its background is in this Farm Holiday?

Oh, no, because there's too much time between and there was too much violence connected with the Farm Holiday, from the economic condition that they were just going to take the law into their own hands. Whereas NFO is doing it more by legislation and trying to enact laws that would be helpful.

Now you knew a lot of these farmers pretty well, didn't you?

Oh, I knew, in those days, every farmer in the county.

Wasn't there a sense of frustration because of the prices?

Yes.

Didn't you have some . . . I don't mean you, but didn't a lot of you people in general have a great deal of sympathy for their cause?

Yes, that's right. Because many farmers couldn't get enough for their products to exist. I can remember, well, I was going to try to find that price. I can give you the prices. The lowest price that I can remember was oats 10 cents a bushel and corn got down to about 15 cents and wheat was around 45 cents. Now compare oats at 10 cents to $1.00 oats today and corn today is about $2.00 and, of course, soybeans were unknown then, no one raised soybeans. I can remember the first soybeans I raised myself; that was in the thirties; we had a very small patch and we didn't know what to do with them after we raised them.

You should have stored them until 1973.

Butterfat was exceptionally cheap and beef was cheap and pork was cheap. I can well remember buying a whole pig for $6.00 that I took north to go hunting with. We used to go north to get a deer and if you took a pork with you, you were bound to bring a deer back whether you shot it or not, because you could always get a deer from the Indians.

For one pig, huh?

Ya, and I remember the old man I bought the pig from. Six dollars for the pig and he butchered it, cut it in two halves. And I gave a half a dollar or so for the cheesecloth I wrapped it in, put it in the trunk of the car and away we went. And pork was down to 2 or 3 cents a pound and good beef on the hoof was 10-12 cents, and a cow, a good milk cow was 10-15 dollars.

So you feel the farmers had a justified reason for feeling frustrated?

Very, very much so. Certainly. As they do now.

What sort of opportunities did they have to redress their grievances? Just pour out in the streets?

Just wait for another crop; starve to death till you got another one. And I'll say this boys, this terror wasn't near as bad as it was west, when you got over in Lincoln and Devel counties.

Or north.

And north, yes. We were in pretty good shape. Nobles County, where Arnold lived, was much better than this county too, although that was higher priced land and they had more debt down there than we did. We had plenty of it.

Do you think farmers generally manage to salvage farms a little easier in Lyon County than they did in Lincoln?

Oh, yes, because we always had more rainfall. And in addition to low prices we had very adverse weather conditions for three or four years. You had conditions there where you didn't have any rainfall and you couldn't raise anything. The only ground in many instances that produced a crop was lake beds and extremely low lands that afterwards had to be drained.

What was your reaction to this incident in Marshall? Did you meet with other county attorneys and talk about these problems? Didn't you have a meeting at Windom once or something right after that?

Yes, we had two or three meetings while it was going on. I went to a meeting and I think Brecht was one of the moving men. And I know I had something to do with organizing the Minnesota Law Enforcement League, or something like that, as we called it. We were intending to put that together and formulate plans for it. But before it really got off the ground the conditions changed. The thing that changed the whole problem was that the legislature was called into special session and Floyd Olson had that legislature enact what was known as a farm moratorium law, where the power or right to foreclose mortgages was all suspended and you had to go into court and get permission to foreclose a mortgage. That moratorium existed for a few months.

Was that a good law?

Well, sure, it helped out to alleviate the distress.

How do you see Olson? Was he a good governor in the sense that he could keep things together?

Oh, he was a master politician. I always thought he was a second Roosevelt when it came to politics. He could make everybody happy and really did make everyone happy. He was a ...

Do you think he would have been a presidential contender had he lived?

Oh, I imagine so. They always talked about it at that time. I stayed with him until the very last year, and then I broke away and went back to the Republican Party but it didn't....

Was there any big thing that caused that?

No.

It's just that you had lived uncomfortably enough for the first ...

By nature, I was a Republican anyway, and I knew that his days were over, and I didn't like his successor or the fellow who was on the horizon then. He was a man from our area, Elmer Benson. He took over and lots of us didn't like him.

But Olson was a very likeable fellow, and I had two or three courses under him in law school.

Did he play both hands against the middle do you think or was he pretty fair with protecting farmers or was he...?

No, he was honest with everyone, just a genuine politician out for votes as every governor was. Stassen was kind of a second Olson so far as we were concerned.

Did they both share that ability to attract members from the opposite party?

Yes, in fact Stassen wanted to get in with Olson before he ran for governor as a Republican.

Did Olson like him?

Oh, I don't know. The story is that he went up to Olson's office and talked to him and Olson said no. Of course, Stassen was in his 20's then and had to wait three or four years after Olson died before he went in. I was in the Stassen campaign actively with him and served in his office a year and a half after he was elected.

Did you know any of the state or national leadership of the Farm Holiday. Did you know John Bosch in Kandiyohi County?

Just by name is all.

He's still alive.

He is? Bosch?

But he was never out here, was he?

No. Siebring, whose first name I can't say, was a dairyman at Granite Falls. He was very active in this territory. He's now dead. He had a dairy farm down along the river and we used to fish when I was, long before I was log specialist official, along the river near his farm. Then I recognized it afterwards. He was the closest of the leaders we ever had much to do with. . . .

But, the foreclosures and the resistance to those foreclosures was quite general. Finally, the last year or two that we had to foreclose mortgages, where we had trouble with getting the sheriff to either perform or where he was prevented from performing, we would start an action in the United States district court for foreclosure and then have the United States marshall conduct the sale and they never bothered the marshall. He would conduct the foreclosure sale and we would get the thing through in that way.

Did you have some specific examples of sales in Lyon County that you had to conduct or resistance to them or any trouble that Mr. Rankin had?

No, I don't think we ever had much trouble with foreclosures in Lyon County. There might have been one or two, not that I had anything to do with. Maybe I had some mixing. I do have remembrance of several in Yellow Medicine County, and several in Chippewa County. Chippewa County was real bad, that was Montevideo. And we had trouble in Madison. Of course, by the time we were getting to the trouble up there as badly as we run into, then we were with the United States marshall. They always went through.

Would that have been '34-'35?

'34, '35, and '36.

Johnson, Ernest C.
S182

NO BIOGRAPHICAL INFORMATION AVAILABLE.

Tell us about the activity of the Farmer's Holiday Association during the 1930's In Watonwan County and Jackson County in Minnesota.

It was our penny sale over there. A fellow by the name of Fry lived on a farm south of St. James, west of Truman. He was renting a farm and in the fall of the year the landlord decided he wanted to move him off. He had a son that got married and he wanted to put him on there. Mr. Fry had a contract that said if he had anything plowed at a certain date that he had the farm rented for another year. But the landlord insisted on moving Mr. Fry out, so he called on the Holiday Association. We met with him several times and tried to make some settlement, and we just couldn't get anywhere with him at all. The landlord was a Board of Director of the Truman Bank and Mr. Fry had his interests in the bank there. It got to be real exciting; we had meeting after meeting clear up to 2 o'clock on the day of the sale. They decided to have the sale. . .well they decided to foreclose him in order to get him off—that was the only way to get him off. They called on the Holiday Association from Iowa to come up. Mr. Fry had a brother-in-law that was an auctioneer who was very sympathetic to the Holiday Association, so we were pretty well set. It was agreed all through the Holiday Association that nobody could bid over a dime on the penny sales on any item. At 2 o'clock the owner of the land, he went out from a porch and said, "I'll take my chances with the Holiday Association." He said, "I've got as many friends out there as the Holiday has." It was estimated that 5,000 people came up from Iowa in order to take part in this sale. We had them all over the state of Minnesota that came in. One lady walked from way up around Madison, hitchhiked down for that particular sale.

The sheriff from Watonwan county, Mr. Brumel, I believe was his name, he came out there, of course, to protect the interest of the bankers, you might say. He set two machine guns up on his big car. This lady from Madison walked up to him and said, "You ain't got the guts to use them even if you had to."

The sale never got on the way until about 2 o'clock in the afternoon; they had sold about half of the machinery, everything selling for anywhere from three, four, five, six cents, somewhere in there. Finally, the banker realized that they were having a legal sale, so he asked the auctioneer, he said, "You mean to say that this is a legal sale?"

He said, "Yes, it is. We advertised it and we are selling to the highest bidder." So the sale went on.

I now want to get down to the horses, They were selling a team there and someone bid twenty cents or something and someone knocked him down that fast. [laughs] When the sale was over, everybody went in and paid up their bill and returned the property to Mr. Fry.

That evening after supper the sheriff from Watonwan County, he deputized all the employees in the highway department and as many people as he could get around town and they came out and took the property to St. James and put it in the fairgrounds. They set up their guards and their machine guns, and defied us to come and get it. Of course we knew better than to go and get it.

So then they decided, the Holiday Association, that they

would make it a test case in the Supreme Court. They called on all the Holiday Associations around to contribute. Within two or three days we had the thousand dollars which it takes to enter a case in the Supreme Court. So they returned the property. We got a bill for $400 for deputy fees and feed, but we haven't paid it yet.

What year was this?

It was in the fall of '32, if I remember correctly. I think it was in the spring of '33 when Governor Olson took the case of foreclosures to the spring court. That was a very exciting sale, went down in history it was the only real penny sale we had here. They had them in other states around, but this was the only one here. We had a lot of strikes and stuff in Minnesota and in Jackson County area that were quite successful, but that is the only penny sale we had that I know of.

You were just kind of rank and file member?

I was, yeah. I did a lot of organizing and working day and night. I know in the Jackson incident down here, when we decided in Lakefield whether we should strike or not, they had set a date to the state that they were going to strike, so we had a meeting at Lakefield and they estimated there were 800 farmers there that night. Charlie Johnson was state president and a fellow named Marshall secretary; they were there. And I remember so well that they discussed for about an hour whether they should strike in the morning. But Charlie Johnson said, "Now, all you fellows that are willing to come down to Jackson in the morning, be there at 7 o'clock and draw your position for the strike, stand up. But if you don't intend to come, for God's sake don't stand up so we know where we are at." And the whole 800 stood up, raring to go, "We'll be there in the morning!" Well, I lived way over south of Mt. Lake about 12 miles; I had about a dozen cows to milk and a lot of chores. I got home that night after twelve and I got up at four, did my chores and made it down to Jackson at 7 o'clock in the morning.

Why did you particularly pick Jackson to start your strike?

Well, it was kind of the center of the whole organization. But this was the sad part: there was 13 of us that showed up out of the 800. I was one of the 13. I drew the Bergen Creamery for my position. We had met with the Creamery board before, and they agreed to close for two or three days if we did strike. They said, "It's your creamery, and if you want to throw your milk away, it's alright with us." Well, I got up there a little bit after eight and many of the people that was at Lakefield the night before— that said, "we will strike and be there"— they come tearing with their milk hoping they could dump it at the creamery before we got striking. They seen they couldn't get away with it, and they couldn't get away with it at Jackson. They had that pretty well sewed up. So they came to Windom here. We had a pretty nice creamery down here and heard that he was buying so much milk and cream that day that 2 o'clock in the afternoon he had to go borrow more money so that he could buy more milk.

So, I called him up. I knew the fellow real well; he had been a friend of mine all my life, I asked him, "Wouldn't you close up just for a day or two and see whether we could make anything out of this?"

"No, sir, I will fight you to a finish, to the last in the state," he said.

"Well," I said, "We will have to call on you."

So we jumped in the car, five of us, and by the time we got there he had told the whole town that the Holiday was coming to wreck his creamery, so we had a lot of company down there. But we discussed with him for about a half hour, and it seemed to be of no use at all, so we went home. We couldn't get any support here in this area, right here anyways. That night we drew places to strike or sit for the evening. I drew Livestock, west of Bergen down there. Another fellow by the name of Harry Olson was with me; he was on the north side and then they had some five or six guys south. I don't remember all the fellows in there. Long about nine o'clock— it was a miserable cold night, it was terribly cold— we were sittin' out there, this man came out and said, "Pretty cold out there fellows, isn't it. You had better come in and have a cup of coffee with us."

We said, "Sure. We have a few other guys down the road that would like to have a cup of coffee too."

He said, "Bring them in." Well, we had plenty of them down there that stayed. He had a lot of trucks, the biggest livestock buyer. We figured he would try to sneak out while we were having a little coffee, so we left some there. We had a lot of planks there with spikes in it. [laughs] We went in and the lady was awfully nice. She gave us an awful nice lunch. We discussed it back and forth, and of course she didn't agree with us on anything. We went back out. The next day we picketed all day. I got the afternoon shift at two. He said he wouldn't even attempt to get out that night.

The next day, George Olson— he was kind of our spokesman, he was our state representative— he said he was going to the city to see if there really was anything doing there. He made a quick trip to the Cities and back, and there wasn't much doing except in the southern tip of the county here. So we gave it up on the third day as sort of a hopeless case.

The livestock man went down to the local paper here, put an article in there telling how he had put it over the Holiday Association, that while his wife was giving us coffee, he snuck out with all his trucks. Well, we had a man on the party line at Bergen's store over there listening, and there was a call that came in after we had lunch for a truck, and he said he just couldn't get out. He said he was picketed on both sides and couldn't get out. That's the way it ended and the paper put it up big. Well, I tried to get a few of the boys to go down and talk to the paper, but we couldn't get anybody to go.

Was the paper just kind of anti-Holiday?

Oh, absolutely, ab-so-lutely.

Was there any kind of newspaper around here that was for the Holiday?

No, I couldn't say there was one here, not a one. There was a few in the state that were sympathetic, but not around here. There was an outlaw who was a member of the organization.

You were farming prior to this time. Did you belong to any farm organizations prior to the Holiday?

I have been in the Farmers Union since it organized. I will have to take you downstairs and show you my work.

We were told the other day— we were down in Worthington talking to Mr. Bill Nystrom— that a lot of people had dual membership in the Farmers Union and the Farmers' Holiday and the union wasn't going to get involved in such radical type activity, so a lot of them had dual membership.

It took a lot of nerve to step right out in the open and fight this way, but there comes a time when you have no other way of fighting back. I think it got so bad that you didn't know whether you was going to live or save the little bit of property and stuff you had. . . foreclosing and everything there was.

Did you own your own farm?

No, I was renting it.

Was there any kind of discrimination shown against you because you were in the Holiday?

Well, yes, but we had a lot of support in here too. We made it kind of rough for some of the businessmen that was anti. We

ERNEST JOHNSON

went in there and the Farm Bureau was terribly close to us at the time. We made some of the business people take their Farm Bureau sign down if they wanted our support. That never sets so good, you know. They were fighting us toenail and teeth. I went fishing in northern Minnesota that next summer and my guide there, he was from LeMars, Iowa, and you know they had a pretty hot spot down there. I got the whole history on that; they really had some experiences down there. He told that on one particular highway to the packing plant there they had it blocked, and when a truck would come they would try to flag them down, and if they didn't stop they slid the planks out. But one day when a truck came down just a-barrelling down the road and the horn blaring all the way, 60 or 70 miles an hour, with a load. She ignored the flag and she ignored the planks, so they dumped a barrel of gasoline on the highway and lit it and she went right through it. She got down a mile or two and all her tires were flat. The boys went down and said, "Anybody that has the nerve to do that, we will fix your tires and give you an O.K. to unload." [laughs]

There wasn't any kind of violence?

No, not here. There was in LeMars, of course. They got pretty rough there. They almost hung the judge there, if you had any information on that. That was on foreclosure of farms in Jackson — I didn't get in on that — but they had two foreclosures on farms there that they stopped. They forced the sheriff off the steps of the court house and, of course, there was no sale. But in LeMars they went so far as to put a rope around his neck and take him out on the lawn. Then they locked up a whole bunch of them, and, of course, the pressure got so terrible all over the United States from the Holiday Association they finally turned them loose. Bill Goede should really give you a lot of information if you keep him on the subject. He likes to get back to sports, fights, and different things he had, you know. No, we done a lot of work on that thing at the time, but the Farm Program was really born out of the effects of the Holiday Association. We would never have had it if we hadn't struck, so we accomplished that much anyway.

Was there a lot of traveling through this area with people like Milo Reno and John Bosch?

Oh, yeah, we had so many meetings with them guys.

They were here quite a lot?

John Bosch spent thousands of dollars, you know. I know at one meeting there he said, "My Dad was in the crowd today; I don't dare tell you how much I spent."

What was your opinion of Milo Reno in comparison to John Bosch?

Oh, I would put Bosch way ahead of Milo Reno. But we didn't have too much meetings or anything with Milo, but with John Bosch we were with him so much.

Did you ever come in contact with A. C. Townley?

No, not directly, but indirectly here. I had a friend south of Mountain Lake. When he got in trouble down in Jackson down there, why he was hiding in that area, and a friend of mine carried food to hi for several days. But they finally caught up with him in Jackson and locked him up. I think that Bill Goede could give you a lot of information about one meeting they had when Charlie Johnson was there. Pretty active out here. They run him out of Jackson and he swam the river.

There has been some indication by various people that the American Communist Party tried to take over the Holiday and organize it as an advanced radical movement.

ERNEST JOHNSON

Oh, pooh, you hear that all the time. Anytime that you oppose a special privilege, why, of course, your branded as communists. That's going on today and it's worse than it was anytime. First there was reds, then they're Bolsheviks, now they're communists.

There has been some indication, though, that the American Communist Party did send some people out here. How successful they were, nobody knows.

At that time I doubt very much that there was; I wouldn't say that now, though. I think there is now, but not at that time, thirty or forty years ago. They had their hands full over there taking care of their own country without meddling in here.

Did you have to pay dues in the Holiday, or how did you work it?

We had a membership. I think it was only a dollar for a member; I have to look. I have one of my cards yet. We had so little money to go with that it was penny here and penny there. We would all chip together and ride in one car with seven or eight in order to get there.

Were you involved in 1933 when they had the big march on the legislature?

You betcha.

Could you tell us a little bit about what happened?

Well, it was a peaceful demonstration, I'll say that —really peaceful. There was a terrific crowd. I had a clipping and a little writing here. Just recently someone wrote up about when the farmers struck in '33 and marched on the Capitol. I put it away, and I looked all day yesterday for it, and I couldn't find it. But anyway, we went up there and we was on the Capitol, of course, by the thousands and thousands.

We had an appointment at 2 o'clock. The Governor came out and talked and we had some delegation from Lakefield on the committee that went in and talked with the legislature. We never got in. We was out on the grounds. But it was a very, very peaceful demonstration. No violence whatever.

I had heard through some newspapermen who were newspapermen at that time that the farmers just went up there and wrecked the place. But I can't very well believe that.

No, it was very peaceful. They have fellows like that all over. Like this cattle man out here west of Bergen, you know. He went into the Cities and deliberately lied, you see, about what happened at his place. He knew better.

You had no way of telling the people?

Well, we would have if I could have got anybody to go along and back up the paper, see, and corrected it, but you can't get them to go. A lot of people hate to step out and tell where they stand, see.

How effective do you think the Holiday was?

Really effective. I remember the President of the United States made a statement there; he said, "If this thing gets worse, we will have to go out and get the food. We are not going to let millions of people starve in the cities on account of a strike out in the country." Which of course is true; they would have to go get it. That's the only thing I heard from the high officials; they were scared. I always said that we would have never got the farm program if it hadn't been for the strike of the Holiday Association.

Then you feel that because of the action of the Holiday, we have some of the farm programs today that the Holiday helped initiate?

ERNEST JOHNSON

Yes, that's right. I don't think it would have ever happened without the Holiday.

How active was the Holiday in politics? Did you try to have anybody run?

No, we really didn't at that time. We hadn't got to the point of organizing our legislatures at all. We were just striving to survive at that time. It was so bad, not only me but any amount of farmers, we had to take a few chickens in at the end of the week for groceries or a few sacks of grain or something, because you couldn't afford to run that old car you had. You couldn't buy gasoline for it. It was really bad, is what it was.

What percentage of the farmers do you feel were like yourself, renters of landowners, that belonged to the Holiday? Do you have any idea what the proportion would be?

No, I don't. But we did have a big group of both because the farm owner was losing his home by foreclosures as well as us renters were starving and trying to stay on the farm. If you got pushed off the farm at that time you were really sunk. You couldn't find no place to work or anything else, you know. It was terrible. I went up to the Cities and down on Washington Avenue and watched them dish out the food to the unemployed there at that time. It was terrible; they had bunks out there like we feed our cattle and they come out there with big things full of sandwiches and stuff. They would all march on both sides and eat it. Later on in the year it got so bad that finally they got a hold of a building where they could pass on through and eat their soup and sandwiches and stuff.

Did the Holiday ever make any effort to get the women involved?

No, I couldn't say they did, but we did have a lot of women. They were involved; they went right along with the men folks. No, we had no effort here at all to get the women involved. They stayed home to take care of the kids.

Yes, I realize that. I thought maybe there might have been some effort to get them involved or some way of trying to help them.

No. There was women that came by the loads just as well as the men folks, but they volunteer by themself. You get the women involved in anything and they can kind of make it go. [laughs] Well, it was a great experience and I wouldn't trade it for anything.

You have said that the Watonwan County and the Jackson County worked together. Was it one unit or was it two separate units?

No, no, no. We were all together, with the Iowa organization too. We had just strings of cars coming a mile long from Iowa on the Holiday Association.

Did you get involved in any of the picketing over in Worthington?

No, I never did.

It has been indicated to me in different areas that they had a training camp over there for picketers. Do you know anything about that?

No, I don't. But I was told that up north some place—I have forgotten the town—where it was quite tense, they had a fellow picketing on the freeway there, on the highway, and one night a bunch of young bucks from town decided to go out there and was going to clear him out. They went out there and they had a .22 rifle along. They started flagging him down and they wouldn't stop so they started shooting. They shot a little too low and shot through the tent and killed the guy.

Was it by Canby?

It could have been, I'm really not sure.

There was a young man killed up by Canby; they were picketing the roads up there and they were out watching at night and some guy came by and just shot at him. They said they were shooting over his head and shot him in the chest.

In Jackson, the sheriff told me himself that he had people coming in there with just big tears in their eyes to be deputized and go out there and just clean us S.O.B.'s out. But he would never deputize them.

Was the sheriff fairly sympathetic?

Yes, he was. He liked to see order instead of conflicts, you know.

How were the rest of the public officials?

Well, of course, we know what they would of liked to do to us. (laughs) We had no sympathy whatever. They figured they could get along without us. There is a little different attitude now; some of these towns realize that they are living off of agriculture. They didn't seem to realize that years ago. Every time we lose a farmer out here now it makes it that much worse for the business people. I see we have lost 23 percent of the farmers of this county in the last ten years; they had the report out yesterday. Just think of it—one fourth. Butz, our Secretary of Agriculture, made a statement here recently that they would possibly eliminate one and one tenth million more farmers until they got it down to where they figure they had enough farmers to run it. . . .

Lots of people have put Governor Floyd B. Olson on a little pedestal as a god or something.

Well, you know, when the moratorium [on farm sales] was declared by the Supreme Court, he was the sole governor of the whole United States that went there. And he said when the trial was over, there was 47 attorney generals sitting clear on the edge of their chair leaning out there to hear that verdict. When it was announced, the next day there was a moratorium over the whole United States. He was the one person in the United States that fought the thing alone. I got to give him a lot of credit for that. And here was the thing: they had no money to refinance all these mortgages in '33 and they was taking them one after the other. Almost right out legally stealing them is what they did. After he declared a moratorium they had all the money you needed to refinance the whole United States. All kinds of ads in the paper and stuff, you know; we even got money to refinance. Why didn't they have it before? People had paid and paid on their farms for 20 or 25 years and had just a few thousand left, you know, and they took it.

Do you feel that some people made money during the depression off of it?

Yes, I know several. They sold their farm and was carrying the mortgage. The guy couldn't pay. I have relatives here over by Heron Lake; they sold a farm to a fellow and they carried the mortgage and he couldn't meet it. They foreclosed on him and they always remark, "We wish there was another one." That's terrible.

Do you feel that it was farmers that took advantage of other farmers?

Oh, just as much as the .... Anybody who was in the position to take it, took it, whether they were a businessman, farmer, or whatever, they took it. Greed rules over everything.

One of the other questions that has been asked was how close do you feel the farmers were during 1932 and 1933 to open rebellion against the government?

Well, we really felt in the fall of '32 that the country was really dangerous. That is what they really felt. At least we felt that way out in the country here. Everybody was up in arms because they were losing their farms, not just by the hundreds, but by the thousands. The renters were hanging on by their teeth and being sold out. It ws really dangerous, is what it was.

You feel that the farmers were really close then to actually getting out the old shotgun.

Yes, we really felt that it was really dangerous at that time. At the penny sale over there by Truman, I had a pretty good idea there what would happen if it got any worse. The guys were so organized there on that penny sale that, like I said, when that guy bid about 15 cents on that team, they knocked him down right there.

Were there any weapons there?

Only the two machine guns, that was all. They belonged to the sheriff. No, there was no weapons, whatever, at that time. It would be different now if something would come up. It seems that almost everybody has got a weapon now, a gun, knife, or something.

They didn't need a gun; they had a pretty big fist?

No, they are so peaceful a group, they don't even lock their houses. Well, I fear for what would have happened if we hadn't got it changed at that time. This country was pretty stirred up. There's nothing more dangerous than hungry people.

Could you say that people like Floyd Olson and Roosevelt saved the country?

Well, I think they saved it from a civil war, that's what I really believe. If it hadn't been for those fellows, why, I fear for what would have happened. You know what Mr. Hoover said to the boys in Washington, for their bonus that time. He chased them all out. They killed quite a few of them. He said they were only a bunch of bums anyways and didn't make any difference.

Farm mortgage foreclosure sale protestants, Madison, Minnesota, March 22, 1933. Donated by Oscar Torstenson.

Haroldson, Clint
S489

Mr. Haroldson was born in Whitfield Township in Kandiyohi County. He attended country school for 8 grades. He worked his way through high school and attended one year of college. Mr. Haroldson was a speaker for the Farm Holiday Association.

Mr. Haroldson, if we could start out this evening by asking you a little bit about your background, where you were born, some of your education, where you were from.

Well, to kind of give you a little background, I was born in Whitefield Township in Kandiyohi County approximately fifteen miles from here. I attended grade school in what was then known as District 55. I went through eight grades there. I stayed home a couple years because my father didn't believe much in going on to further education, but then I got the idea that I wanted a little education. So, I left home and went out and got a job at fifteen years of age, as a full-time hired man then. Well, I worked and I suppose like young fellows, you don't save anything, but I went to school anyway. I struck off for Willmar, the high school there, and fortunately after a week I got a job. This is how I worked my way through high school. I did it in three years. At the time, I thought I was busy: I sang with two church choirs, two male choruses, the Legion. I participated in oratory and the base solo in chorus in high school. So I was busy besides working. Well, following that, I graduated in 1928. Then of course I thought in terms of college, but not having much support . . . I did go one year to college at St. Peter, I suppose because my buddies went there. I had scholarships for other colleges but never used them. Well, following that year, I suppose you could say that beginning of the depression was coming. Well, I didn't get back to college, and then it was a matter of finding what jobs you could. In fact I worked out in North Dakota and I sold canned fruit. I did a little of everything. The winter I went to the Cities. I suppose I might say I had the most menial job in Donaldson's Department Store: I bailed paper. Well, this went on then until I think it was in '32. I had worked for various farmers in between times and various jobs. Then in, I think it was 1932, a gentleman by the name of John Bosch came to the school house which was our local gathering place in Svea, and approached a few of us young fellows. We thought we were liberals. And he talked over this thought of having a farmers' strike. The people who were at that meeting were Rueben Felt, Fillmore Nelson, Maynard Haraldson, and myself, Harold Peterson, Billie Hillman. Mr. Bosch explained this thought of having a farm strike. Well, it took hold, and that evening during his discourse to the Farmers Union meeting, he mentioned the possibility of a strike. Like a young upstart, I had to get in and say something too. Well, this in essence as far as I know, was the original concept of how the Holiday started.

Well, I was working at the time for one of my parental neighbors, on a farm, and of course because of the beginning of the Holiday, I was interested to see what would happen. I think it was in August, I told my employer that I was going to quit. This was right in the middle of harvest, yet I quit because I thought I am going to get in touch with this Holiday movement. I joined with John Bosch; in fact, I was his flunkie, I did much of the driving. Then, of course, there were so many requests for meetings and for organizational work that John couldn't make all of them, so he enlisted this young Peterson, Harold Peterson, and myself to go on our own, the two of us presenting the Holiday Association approach. One of us would give the statement, or the principles of the Holiday and show the general need of it, and the other fellow would show the need for a cost-of-production position. So we divided up the responsibilities and we made many of the meetings. Of course in the mean time John Bosch and Hemming Nelson, who was a former legislator from Lake Lillian area — Kandiyohi County, but lived in Lake Lillian — also made many meetings. The request for meetings grew so rapidly that Harold Peterson and I did many of them. I would say it would be in the southeastern part of the state that we went. Well, following that, I don't know for what reason, but Peterson had to remain at home and there was a person from Montevideo, Minnesota — I can't recall his name anymore — he offered his car and a driver, so that we could continue the efforts of the Holiday Association. Well, then I became the so-called individual that was supposed to go with this person . . . we started working to the north and northeast part of Minnesota, holding meetings explaining the Holiday Association and the cost of production. I then took both aspects of the presentation.

One little incident I have to recall, because I admit I was real nervous. There had been a meeting at Little Falls, sort of an organization meeting, not totally successful in the extent that a good organization was not set up. So there was an agreement that we should return again to Little Falls. The meeting was set up, and when I arrived in town I was told that the truckers were going to boycott the meeting. In fact, they were going to run me out of town. Boy, for a young upstart, I was nervous, believe me. Well, anyway, with this knowledge presented to me, I started out my talk and I went through. In fact, I have to admit I transgressed as a public speaker: I talked for three hours, and that is unforgivable. The hall was packed and I envisioned that around the edges were all the truckers waited to heckle me and more or less break up the meeting, but evidently, those farmers who were concerned stayed and asked questions. Evidently the truckers decided it was of little avail and one by one they left the hall. In fact, we set up a good organization in that county.

Well, we made many meetings following that and one of the little incidents I remember is we were working north. One Saturday evening we came to Walker, Minnesota. I don't recall just what we had done during the day — I presume we had been arranging for future meetings — but anyway, when this fellow and I arrived in Walker the day was spent, so we went to eat, which was proper I presume. But anyway, after paying for the meal I think I had something like twenty-five cents left in my pocket. Collections had not been so good as of the past few meetings. Well, I suppose I had a little gambling instinct, because after finishing my meal I turned around right behind me were some slot machines. I thought, well heck, you are darn broke, I will put in a nickel. I got a dollar and a quarter back. Well, I thought I had better take it off that, so I put in another nickel and I got the jackpot. That evening, there was nothing to do as far as the Holiday Association was concerned, so I went about town and there were slot machines in practically every place in town, and I watched the young folks play these slot machines until they had filled them up, and when they quit I would play them until I broke them. In fact, that night I broke nine slot machines, clearing thirty-seven dollars and some cents. That's what we had to run on for awhile.

Was that man's name from Montevideo Harry Haugland?

No, it wasn't Harry Haugland. Harry was very active in the Holiday Movement, but it was not Harry Haugland.

I just thought it might have been him. Were there any Holiday organizations in the county that were organized that were not sanctioned by the state organization?

None that I would know of. In fact, as the movement grew... I suppose one should refer to some of the incidents relative to it to show how the Holiday movement grew. For example, in Kandiyohi County because John Bosch was busy organizing all over the state and probably part of the nation, there came a situation of a foreclosure sale. This one, I happen to remember, was a gentleman living over in the Atwater area. He didn't have the where-with-all to pay his mortgage when it was due, and the bank was to foreclose on him. Well, it happened to be that John asked me to go there and try to negotiate with them. Well, in the meantime, there had been other foreclosure sales in various places in the state in which the farmers in the community felt that the debtor still had a large equity in there. They would hold what they call a one-cent sale. They would gather together, get close around the auctioneer, in fact, they would pack so tight that any outside bidder's bid couldn't be heard, and various items would sell for one, two, or three cents. Of course with no more bids, the auctioneer had to sell. Then these farmers would just turn back the property to him. Well, based on this assumption, that it could happen, I then negotiated with the banker and this farmer to have them postpone this particular sale. It was successful because this fellow in years to come did pay off his indebtedness when prices got better.

One other incident in Kandiyohi County I remember very vividly, because in this case, this farm that was to be foreclosed on was a farm, as I recall, in Lake Lillian Township. The indebtedness was not, I should say, probably less than half of the equity left in the farm, but because the farmer couldn't raise any money to pay off the mortgage at that particular time this bank decided they were going to foreclose. See, to have a farm foreclosure sale, the sheriff would have to sell the property on the front steps of the courthouse. That's the only legal spot on which it can be done. Well, the farmers gathered and stopped the foreclosure sale. Well, they were still determined they were going to do it, so they set an additional date at which they were going to sell this farm. The farmers in the community, of course, were pretty darn mad. They should have been satisfied that they stopped once, but they insisted on it. As I recall, on that day six hundred farmers gathered in the Willmar courthouse — that's in the old courthouse — and we in fact had the place jammed. The halls were full, and people outside. To many people the intent was to jam the hall so much that the sheriff, then Paul Anderson, a large person, couldn't get out of his office much less get to the front steps. Well, because he was a large man he did work his way through the halls, and he would push, and he would once in a while say "excuse me," I don't recall for sure. He did work his way through the hall toward the front steps. I recall an incident right there very vivdly because at that time he came between me and a gentleman from Atwater, this fellow, believe me, was mad. He looked up to Paul — I say looked up because he was shorter than the sheriff — and he said to him, "If you move one step further you will land on Boot Hill." You know, I was scared. But the sheriff stopped right there and there was no foreclosure sale. That's one of the incidents that happened here and I suppose while I am speaking of incidents of this nature, I would relate one of that I was told about. I wasn't there personally; I was told by a person who I thought was reliable.

As I recall this incident happened in Lac Qui Parle County, where a similar situation occured where a farmer couldn't pay his indebtedness on a mortgage [both personal property and real estate] and the intent of the bank was to foreclose. The farmers did gather and stopped the sale. Well, this particular situation was grave to the extent that the mortgage holder decided that, by gosh, he was gonna foreclose this thing, period. And he enlisted the aid of a federal marshall to sell the property at this farm. Well, this had to be advertised, of course, and the whole community gathered. In fact, that farm yard was just packed with people, not just men but women as well. When the federal marshall drove up to the place, got out of his car and proceeded to the spot where he was going to start the auction, one man — not a large man — stepped up in front of him and he said to the federal marshall, "Give me your gun." The federal marshall stopped and was about ready to reach for his gun and order this guy out of the way, but he took his gun out of his holster and handed it over to the guy. Now that, I presume, would show how intent these people were. If that federal marshall had shot this man, he would have never lived.

Do you think the situation was such that there would have been mass . . . ?

There would have been murder there, if you want to call it that, because they wouldn't have stood for it. They would have, I am quite sure, I was told, have seized him and probably angry enough to tear him limb from limb.

The fact of shooting him would have just sparked a riot?

Oh, it would have been a riot.

Was there any real violence other than things like this? Was there any violence at these penny auctions where somebody would bid things up that you know of?

I wasn't at any of them because I was usually out organizing, but from what I was told, once in a while there would probably be a few violent statements made, not complimentary, and probably a fist or two swung once in a while, but that was the extent of it.

Just little fisticuffs?

Yes, because the usual thing that happened was that the neighbors would gather so close to the auctioneer that any outside bidder was so far away that he was out on the fringe. There would probably be, oh, three or four hundred people gathered around the auctioneer. It was going to be one cent sale, period.

Were there any women's organizations developed with the Farm Holiday?

Not of any major development as I recall. I think at one time there was an attempt to organize an auxiliary, and I think there were a few meetings, but I don't recall any specific. When you speak of violence, one incident I suppose you can say bordered on this violence, was east of Willmar, when the Holiday group of Kandiyohi County was trying to stop truckers from hauling the livestock. This strike was to withhold farm produce, and some of the truckers, of course, wanted to haul. That's how they made their money. They gathered and tried to stop them. Some of them would go through, so some guy concocted the idea to drive spikes in the plank. What they would do, would try to hail the trucker down to stop him, but if he came barelling as though he was going to go through, they would shove the damn plank out. A few tires were punctured, admittedly. Well, there was one instance — I wasn't there but it happened — that I was told about it: this trucker, who had his tires punctured with one of these, got out and he took a swing at one of these fellows. Well, this fellow had a little hot temper too, and he returned the swing. Well, there was pretty good fisticuffs, and the result of it was that they filed suit against them for some reason. They had a court trial. It didn't amount to too much. I guess the fellow who assisted in shoving the plank out and who was also in on the fisticuffs got a small sentence. It wasn't of any major consequence.

Were these farmers willing to accept that type of thing? Did they realize that they were in a way breaking the law? Were they willing to face the consequences for the cause?

I think some of them would have. I think they would have gone. The emotions, if I can use that term in this case, were so great, because prices being so depressing, they couldn't pay their indebtedness. In fact, they couldn't continue their operation without having to try to get additional funds. Of course, then they couldn't pay their debts, and I presume when you are faced with the possibility of loosing your home or loosing your farm and all, and you have a family, you get pretty darn desperate. I don't blame them because, sure, they might have five, six, or seven kids in this family. Where would they go? There were no jobs to be had. I would say some of them, not all, but some would have gone to quite some degree to protect that which they had, and they thought this was the vehicle they could use. The essence of striking to withhold the produce was probably the first concept of it, but then when the foreclosures came into the picture and the stopping of foreclosures. The essence of the movement got to be deterring foreclosures.

So then, the aim and objectives of the organization had changed?

It shifted sort of, I would say.

Do you feel then that the stopping of the foreclosures was the more important part of the overall Holiday activity?

In a manner, and yet I would say that it couldn't have started in that way. The fact of withholding the products to give the first incentive to try to increase the price was a natural from a standpoint that these farmers, I would say 99.99% were willing and wanted to pay their debts, but they didn't have the money. So they would join based on this. Then these other developments came, so I would suppose you could say it is sort of a transition.

How successful or how united do you think the farmers were on withholding or the strike aspect of the organization? Do you think it was well organized or were you still suffering from organization growing pains?

Well, I suppose you can say it was successful partially because I think a certain percentage — and I don't know that I would want to venture an exact guess — of the people who would withhold voluntarily. You always find in the human race some fellow that feels that based on this, I am going to take an extra nickel or dime, and then he tried to run his produce through. This, I think, is how you find it today too. This was a deterrent to the total success. In fact, if I recall one of the statements that we made at that time, if the farmers had withheld their produce totally, within one week the rest of society would have been without food. Well then, of course, they would wake up to the plight. But of course, there was always a dribble in, so that food did move. I would repeat again that it wasn't totally successful, and yet, it had the effect that the people in the cities and in government became aware of the acuteness of the situation.

You feel more that the effect of it was more important than the original objectives?

Yes, I think that's true.

Did you then feel that at this time — now this was shortly after this whole thing had been organized — that sort of brought all these farmers together underneath an umbrella of hope?

Oh, I think this is true. Well, the situation became so acute that when you think in terms of probably somewhere from 25 to 50 percent of the people were in danger of loosing their way of life. The others who probably weren't in that financial condition, but saw what was happening to their neighbors, became sympathetic. This is I think, is the reason for the success. The sympathy of the neighbors towards their fellow man, with the essence of being told down the road, we don't need you.

Was there, during the time when you were out organizing, any organized effort to discredit you or the Farm Holiday Movement by other farm organizations?

Oh, as far as I was personally concerned, no. There wasn't any attempt that I know of to try to discredit my little part in it. I didn't feel that. I don't know that any farm organization did make any special effort. Oh sure, there was probably some statement by some official, but it was not a unified effort. I would say this: individuals here and there would try to discredit, oh, that bunch of radicals, law-breakers . . . you hear those today.

There were some farmers and some small groups that did come to heckle and discredit?

Oh surely, and then they would use the media to try to discredit this so-called bunch of radicals. That's just normal I guess. There was a certain amount of that, but not any unified effort that I recall. Of course, remember I was just a young fellow. I didn't get in on everything.

When you were going out and seeing these farmers at different organization meetings, in your opinion, what type of farmers were joining the organization? Where did they fit in the economic scale of rural agriculture? Were they at the top, middle, bottom?

Well, I would say if we think of them politically, approach it that way first, I would say that they were probably more of the liberal aspect. I wouldn't call them a total conservative, although I do recall even in our county here, some people that I would today call a very conservative political person who then participated in the Holiday. I can't tell you why, except it was that feeling of my neighbor facing this situation. As fas as their condition in the economic scale, oh, I suppose you would have to say they were in the lower 50 percent, because normally those were the people who didn't have a backlog of any savings, if there were any. I suppose you can say all men are supposed to be equal, but we differ in our abilities, and some of them just happened to have the ability to gather in more money or produce more. I suppose you would have to say on the economic scale, they were from the 50 percent down.

Most of these then were . . . could most of these be young farmers just getting started?

Well, I wouldn't say that it was this totally, no. Because when I refer to this earlier incident, this farmer had farmed for many, many years.

Of course, there are exceptions to the rules.

But I would generally say, it was about 50/50, young and older people.

Pretty much straight across the board?

Pretty much straight across the board. You know, I was thinking of another thing as we are visiting. See, outside of my organizing, I traveled with John Bosch a lot because he was on demand for speaking engagements, and you cannot drive all day and most of the night and keep up. So I became his driver in essence. I recall one incident: he was requested to be up in Kanabec County for a talk in the afternoon; that evening we had to go clear across the state to Clay County and then get home that night because he had to be in another place the next morning. In fact, we drove as fast as that old Model A could go, and John, because he was tired, left the driving to me. I recall when we were going along, I suppose breakneck speed at the time, I met a car on a bridge and because we were hurrying I suppose I didn't use the best judgement and I would swear that when I met that car on the bridge there wasn't two inches between our vehicles. Oh gad, after that I decided I had better slow down. That was just one of the hair-raising incidents. But many times when I traveled with John, we wouldn't get home until three o'clock in the morning. We would go to bed, get a little rest, and many times we were on the road again at six o'clock in the morning. It was fatiguing at times.

What kind of a man was this John Bosch?

Well, I had a great deal of admiration for John. In fact, not because I am distantly related to him, but John had in my opinion a good analyical mind. He had the capacity to read and to gather information that he would read. He could analyse well and as far as I felt at that time— I still feel strongly that way— [when] John presented these conditions to the average person, it was a pretty sound presentation. I thought he did exceptionally well. Of course, he and I had a lot of fun together because as we drove one of us would take the opposite side of a question, just to bring up an argument, and we would do this for miles. Personally I thought John had a real good analytical mind.

Do you feel then that he was a good leadership person for the Minnesota organization?

Yes, in many ways except for probably one little criticism that I would have. He felt so strongly that the organization should succeed that he sometimes as state chairman— see he was elected state chairman— probably didn't wield, say, a sort of control. I wouldn't say that things got out of line very far, but once in a while there would probably be a little incident that should have been controlled a little more closely. But that would be the only criticism that I would have, because as far as conducting the state organization and its organization and approach to the governor and then later to the Congress, I thought John did very well. When the approach came to the federal Congress of the United States, Milo Reno, who was national chairman at that time, participated in that part.

What kind of a relationship was there between Milo Reno and John Bosch?

As far as I know, it was very congenial, friendly. The only thing I would say in this regard as a young person at that time, I felt as though John Bosch should have been the national chairman. Milo Reno was a very effective speaker and I presume he followed the Holiday philosophy well, but he was chosen as the national president and . . . of course, I suppose I had a little prejudice, because I thought John should have. I didn't know Milo Reno near as well as John, of course; my association was limited in that respect. I didn't get outside the state in the organization work or the travels much, except when I would sometimes drive out of state for John Bosch.

Do you feel then that John Bosch was pretty well accepted statewide as the leader?

Oh, I think so, very definitely. And his association with Governor Olson, I thought, was exceptional. In fact, even though the Governor was probably busy and we would come to town in a situation where it was unannounced, Governor Olson's door was open to John Bosch anytime he wanted to come.

They worked pretty closely together then on trying to resolve the problems?

I think so. I felt as though Governor Olson was very sympathetic to the needs of the farm people.

This is getting off the subject a little, but I want to ask you this question about Governor Olson. How far do you think he would have gone if he had not died? In his political career?

Yes, when you consider national politics, that's quite a business. I felt as though Olson had . . . well, I suppose you could use the term, made an impression on the voters that he could have been elected to another term as governor if he had chosen. He had an unusual capacity for meeting people and remembering them, and this is a gift. When people would come to his office and tell of their situation, their depressing condition, if he would meet them somewhere else he could call them by name. Well, that's a great attribute in politics. I recall an incident where he had walked into a meeting and people who he had seen previously. He would call them by name, go right down the line, you know. The fact that he took his position both for organized labor and for the farmers, I think he could have been elected again. Now to speculate whether he would have been president . . . I don't know, it may have been possible.

Did you ever get the impression, or even hear anybody say that the Holiday was just promising the farmers the end of the rainbow, just leading them down the primrose path, they were promising them the moon, that they were never going to . . . .

Oh, I suppose you could say there were a few. There might have been a few of them, but that was very limited because— actually I am speaking from just memory of course— but many merchants faced the possibility of losing their business because the farmer didn't have the wherewithal to do much purchasing and I think many merchants were in total sympathy. Probably some of them would say, "Oh, a bunch of radicals." But, by gosh, they were looking forward to the day when the old cash register would ring too. So I would say, of course I speak of the areas which I either lived or worked in; I can't say for the whole state, because I wasn't there.

What was your general consensus of the effectiveness on kind of an overall type thing to the actions of the Farm Holiday?

Well, I think I would say that because of the impression that the Holiday organization, or the act of striking, had created an awareness by the governments, state and federal. I think the Holiday organization was successful from the standpoint that I personally believed that because of this, we did get state and federal legislation which then put a moratorium on foreclosures, a moratorium for a specified period. It occurred within our state and I am quite sure it occurred in other states, and I am not just sure but I think it was in 1934, the Congress of the United States enacted legislation which put a moratorium, in essence, on foreclosures when the equity in a piece of property or real estate was such that it was warranted. This gave then, I presume you could say, the position that you would provide credit to the depressed farmers so that they could withstand this depression until prices became on the increase. I suppose this partially developed because... well, as I recall, the depression was in its depth say, from '31 on up to '35 and '36. This is probably sad to say, but at that time the military conflicts of the world started to develop, and it always seems that when you have a world conflict of some nature, prices go up, and of course then when they upgraded the prices, these people realized the income, and of course they then paid off their mortgages. I don't suppose they paid off every last dime, but [it got] them into the position where foreclosures were not as evident. I am probably bringing in world politics and so forth.

No, I think that has a very important part of it, because it seems that at the start of the Second World War or events up to it, the farm situation kept improving and kept going up.

It did.

And with the need for food the world over, the farms products were saleable again and as soon as they were saleable again, they could afford to raise a crop and they could afford to sell it, and of course as soon as they could sell it at a profit they could then afford to go pay their bills, and they could afford to go and buy more things.

True. And I think this works right hand in glove with the idea that with the increased demand for military materials, the non-agricultural person gets a job. They spent money and of course then that brings up the farm prices.

Thompson, Gordon
S177

Gordon Thompson served as the City Clerk of Worthington, Minnesota from 1935 until 1969.

Were you familiar with some of the farm difficulties of that period, foreclosures and loss of farms?

The farm problem was that even if they had a good crop, the price was depressed so much that even if they had a real good yield, why they didn't get too much money. And then they still had to periodically replace their equipment and continue to live and take care of their buildings on the place. So they suffered. Of course one of the things in which I think probably the farmer had the advantage over the city people was that in those days most of them had chickens, cows, hogs and everything else, so that they got a good deal of their food off the farm and had that start over us city people at least, because we didn't have that. But there again I think most of the people in those days had gardens and got a lot of their product out of the gardens, as much as they could. But generally the depression didn't play any favorites; it took everyone involved.

How widespread do you recall the Farm Holiday Movement being here? Was it pretty strong?

At one time it was fairly strong. I remember at one time the sheriff was called down. I think people were trying to haul their animals to Sioux City or Omaha, Sioux City possibly. A bunch of farmers . . . we have an underpass down in the southwest part of the city here, and traffic from the city goes out and south towards Sioux City. There were a bunch of farmers that had met down there that were going to stop this caravan of trucks from going down to Sioux City, and they had to have the sheriff come down there, and luckily he was a pretty forceful individual by the name of Eldon Rowe. He managed to get the group broken up without any bloodshed or anything, so it wasn't as serious evidently as it was in some of the other places. But I think possibly could have been.

How do you describe Mr. Rowe as being forceful? Is there anything you recollect personally about him? He was pretty prominent in some of those activities I guess.

He . . . there again I was younger and fortunately was never involved with the sheriff [laughter]. But from what I saw in my own observation and what the people said, he evidently must have been a pretty fair person. Which is a good background for anything, I guess. But he could be firm when something was not according to the law. He could explain it to the people and tell them that he was going to have to enforce the law as it was. He must have been a man of his convictions and also was able to convince the people that he was, because it finally came down to which way do you go: do you go by what the law says or do you try to go against it? He was fortunate or good at his job, one or the other, because he did manage to keep them from getting out of hand in most of the occasions that arose there. There were very few instances where he didn't.

Do you recall a lot of the pressure from the northwest Iowa farmers coming into this region? They were a little more violence-prone weren't they?

I think they were involved in this one down at the corner of the city here. But I think also there were farmers from the general area, and probably just as it is today, the agitators come, a few, from a greater distance to help stir up the situation. I think it was probably the same thing then.

What Minnesota programs—for instance Olson's administration, Governor Floyd Olson— were there any Minnesota programs that particularly helped Worthington in the depression, or were they pretty much under local goverment?

I think most of the programs, at least the ones that I knowledge of, were federal programs. Basically, I think the state was in about the same position that the rest of the local county and municipal governments were in. They didn't have an excess of money and were depending on the federal government also.

Photo courtesy S.S.U. Southwest Minnesota Historical Center.

Gold, D.W.
S199
March 23, 1973

Donald Gold was born in Sacred Heart, Minnesota in 1893. His family moved to Renville when he was very young and his father was a banker. They then moved to Redwood Falls, MN where he finished high school. Donald served in WWI in the tank corps. He worked for the Mutual Benefit Life Insurance Company during the Depression.

So you must have been handling farm loans, then, during the tough times of the twenties and thirties?

Yes, the Joint Stock Land Bank quit when I went to work for the Mutual Benefit Life Insurance Company on November 1, 1934. They own, I think, around 600 farms here in Minnesota. They had made a terrific blunder in making those loans that they got those farms. They loaned many millions of dollars in 1919, and '20, and '21, when this land went way up. Very, very foolishly, they made all five-year loans, just for five years, with no required payment on principal . . . no required payment on the principal. And I had a guy down near Rochester later tell me that he tried to pay something on the principal of his loan. They wouldn't take it. "We don't want the money." At the end of five years, the land wasn't worth as much as it had been when that loan was made. The loan was still as big. They had paid a big commission to get the loan, and they were going to have to pay another commission to get a renewal of the loan. A lot of them just said, "the heck with it, take the farm." So that's why they got all of this land. They hired a bunch of us guys to manage these farms for them; plant the crops on them, rent them, repair them, and sell them. Then in the late thirties, when we had the land all sold, early forties, we started making farm loans again for the Mutual Benefit Life Insurance Company. We were making twenty-year loans, with a required principle payment every year. It was a fairly full loan. We ballooned those payments a little bit at the start, a little bigger for the first few years, to get them down. A company doesn't acquire farms on that kind of a loan.

Now in the thirties when these companies got these farms, they must have lost a bundle selling them . . .

Some of them, but they went up. I think by the time the thirties came along, they were up enough that they came out fairly well. Because that was a fairly conservative first mortgage that they had made back there in the early twenties. Not too bad, but if they'd have sold them in the late twenties, yes. But they made, in the thirties when I was helping them sell them. . . I've forgotten the exact details. But we would sell those farms with a very small payment down, and five years on a contract for deed. You'd pay for five years, and then, when you had to cut down some more, then you got a deed to it. My golly, I think the first two years, or three years, they paid about three percent interest and then four and five. They had very liberal terms. I didn't buy any of them!

What was your attitude towards these efforts, like the Farmers' Holiday Association to stop those land foreclosures?

I think they were wrong. I can tell you a little experience about that. We had a loan on a farm up near Wood Lake, Minnesota. The farm was owned by a veterinary doctor, in Wood Lake, and rented out. The farm wasn't bringing in much, and he had . . . I've forgotten just what kind of a deal he made, but he had turned that farm over to the company. Not deeded it to them, but let them manage the farm and collect the net income from the farm and apply it on the mortgage, interest and so on. We were managing the farm. I was up there collecting the rents off of them, and so on. Then, sometime after I went to work in '34, he all of a sudden went out and collected a year's crop off of it and refused to turn it over. So the company started foreclosure. What else could they do? He'd broken his agreement. The only thing we could do was to start foreclosure on him. So we did.

In Yellow Medicine County it was quite notorious for that. The sheriff—I've forgotten his name, but I met him—was elected by this Farm Holiday group. He was right hand in glove with them. So this farm was supposed to be put for sale on a certain date up in Granite Falls. They asked the newspaper publisher there in Granite Falls, who would publish the foreclosure notice, to go up and bid it in. They wouldn't let him bid it in. So he got scared of it. Thought they might come down and wreck his printing plant. So I was told to go up there. I went up and went to the sheriff's office in Granite Falls. The thing was supposed to be sold at 10:00 in the morning, and there were three or four heads of the sheriff and three or four heads of the Farmer's Holiday Association in that office, and a half dozen cars outside full of guys. It came time and they made no attempt to sell it. The sheriff just said, "Well, call the office in Minneapolis and tell them the sale can't be held."

So I called up the office, and H.F. Williams was in charge of it. I told him the sale couldn't be held. Well, he says, "What's the matter with those guys? How many guys are there?" "Oh, enough to stop it," the sheriff said; "it can't be held." And the sheriff said, "See if he won't extend it." For it had been extended for a week at a time here, they just extended for one week and then held another sale. They had to come in again. So, "ask them if they won't extend it for a month this time, and these guys are too busy to come in."

So I told H.F. that over the phone, but he was smart enough. "No, sir, you tell them that sale will be held every Friday, or whatever it was until Christmas." So that was that. Well, then I told those people, "Our company wants to be fair. If Doctor so and so"— I've forgotten his name—"would be fair with us, we'd be fair with him. He assigned that farm to us. That crop belonged to us. He took the crop and kept it. What else could we do? If he turned the crop over, they'll go back to this arrangement again. But if he don't, what can we do but foreclose? You're not . . . he didn't . . . play fair with us at all, and I think you fellows want to be fair."

Well, the foreclosure did go through the next time then, but we had another loan on a small farm up near Echo, and the people still lived on it. They called me up there one time, and that wasn't in foreclosure at all. But they said that sheriff of the Yellow Medicine County came in to see them. He said, "If the Mutual Benefit starts foreclosure of this thing, you let me know, and we'll stop the sale." The sheriff went out and did that!
And one more story about that. There's a farm that comes onto Highway 71, this side of Olivia, Breitkreutz, and golly, in 1935, I loaned him money, a company did, on seed grain note, and bought seed for him. We had a loan on the farm, and then all of a sudden he decided he was gonna let that go to foreclosure. And he told me, "Go ahead and foreclose, I'm not gonna pay another thing on it." So the company started foreclosure. Then he changed his mind again. He didn't say anything to us, but he put in an application with the Federal Land Bank in Olivia to get a loan on it to pay us off. The guy that took the application up there, the secretary of the association, he just stuck it in his pocket and collected the fee. Stuck it in his pocket, and never said anything to the Federal Land Bank. This Breitkreutz, he wanted to get a commitment from the Federal Land Bank before he let the sale be held. It really didn't make any difference, as far as he was concerned, whether the sale was held or not. If he could refinance it, why, he could do that after the sale or anytime. But he didn't know that. You couldn't tell him that. So he went to the Farm Holiday there in Renville County and asked them to stop that sale. I heard about it, so I went to the sheriff in Renville County up there and told him, "they're going to stop this Breitkreutz's sale."

He says, "they've never stopped one on me here yet, and by golly, they're not going to stop this one."

But they did. The sheriff's office was on the second floor of the court house in Olivia. Before that sale was to be held at the front door of the court house, say, at 10:00 in the morning, or 9:00, before that time came, that hallway and stairway was just packed solid with farmers. The sheriff just absolutely could not get out of his office and out the front door to hold that sale. So that was stopped. I think it was stopped twice. Word went back to the home office. Meantime, that application had gone in to the Federal Land Bank and they had made a commitment and the home office got quite worried about it. But I told them it will be stopped once more and then he'll get a commitment and then they'll let the sale go through. That's what happened, and we acquired the farm and sold it back to him. I think he still owns it.

Did you know of any cases where people were trying to make payments and simply couldn't make them? Was your company inclined to leniency?

They didn't want these farms.

So they would have done anything, in your mind, to stop...

That's right.

They didn't want to foreclose.

It's a good point, because a lot of people have an image of these bankers and insurance companies just waiting to grab up these farms, just wanting to get them. I never did think that was quite right in terms of the business aspect of it. I don't think the insurance companies make money that way. When I went to work for the Mutual Benefit in 1934, they had a loan on a farm just south of U.S. 12 and two, three miles east of the village of Kandiyohi, up in Kandiyohi County. He was delinquent, as most of us were. I went there to see him and he was coming along pretty good. We worked along and never did foreclose on that one.

But I had forgotten that there was another farm. A year or two ago, shortly before Christmas one evening, there was a knock at our front door. Our front door bell rang, and I went there. There was a middle-aged man and his wife. He says, "I'm,"— what was that name, anyway?— "I'm the son of this man that had the farm up there, on . . . ."

I said, "I remember your father and that farm up there."

And then he reminded me that they had another farm that he was farming, this young fellow was farming. The man that had been there for the company ahead of me, had recommended foreclosure on that one. But I came along and checked into it and suggested to the company to give them a little more time. They did give him a little more time and he managed to catch up. He still owns that farm. And, by golly, he was here in town that evening just a year or two ago, having dinner. He said he'd always had in mind, if he got out to Redwood Falls, to find out if I was still there. He wanted to thank me for what I'd done for them way back in 1934. He came. He was so thankful. He sure appreciated it. He's done very well up there. He owns quite a lot of land, and he's very comfortably fixed.

Excuse me. Did the insurance companies change their policies on foreclosures from, say, '29 to '33, when things started getting worse?

Well, we weren't making any loans then, but they still had some of these loans. They were riding along the very best they could. They had all the farms they wanted. They didn't want any more.

Do you think most of them were like this, or just the one you represented?

Oh, I think so.

Why do you think there was such an intense movement then? Were the farmers just given bad information, or why were there so many that reacted?

Well, at the end of World War I rent went up tremendously around here. My older brother, when I got home from the army in 1919, in August, he'd bought and sold several farms and owned some farms. I had nothing and I was kind of unhappy about that. But, two, three years later, when he was scratching to dig up interest to pay on them, I was glad he had the farms and I didn't. Because the price had jumped up fast and then dropped off rather fast.

So you think that left farmers holding the bag?

That's right.

So you think they formed the Farm Holiday as a means of . . .

That's right.

Salvaging what they could?

Yes, yes.

So you don't feel hostile about those farmers that join the Farm Holiday?

Some of them were all right. Some of them were very radical: A man like this sheriff up there, that would go to people that weren't in trouble and offer to stop a mortgage foreclosure if they ever did get in trouble. And here was a public official that was in there to uphold the law. That I didn't agree with. But the other guys, yes.

Johnson, William
S197

William Johnson was the editor of the Ivanhoe *Times* from 1906-1951. He was born in Marshalltown, Iowa on August 14, 1884. He moved to Lincoln County, Minnesota when he was 6 years old.

There got to be quite a few foreclosures that swept the country. So these Holiday Associations, what they did for them was that they tried to stop them by means of coming around the day before the sale. And they would come, they did to Ivanhoe and I guess elsewhere, they'd generally come in four or five truckloads . . . they'd have a wagon box with sideboards . . . and there would be four or five of those trucks that would come in. Suppose the sale was 10:00 in the forenoon, and they'd drive into the main street of Ivanhoe not later than 9:00, and they'd start to unload and walk around and, of course, they were all strangers. There wasn't anyone around Ivanhoe and Lincoln County, hardly anybody. There might have been a few scattered, but very few; they were from outside—Lac Qui Parle, Yellow Medicine—or some other community. But anyway they were all strangers and would walk around. When it came around the time of 10:00, of course, I would come and get up and represent the mortgagee at the sale. At the hour of 10:00, you know, we were just at the front, the sheriff and I, and the sheriff would start to read the notice of sale, and he got about a half a paragraph and three or four of these big guys they just grabbed him. The first time they ever did that it really created quite a lot of excitement; as far as I was concerned, I never seen anything like it. They grabbed that man, the sheriff—he was about six foot three or four and he weighed 240 or 250 pounds, about 52 or 53 years old, a big strong husky man, but he had no chance at all. They grabbed him by the arms and legs and they just shoved him down the hallway, down into the lower offices downstairs and took him down in the corner and shoved him down in a chair, and said, "And you stay there." And just stood around and watched him. They'd keep him there an hour. Well, after the hour from 10:00 to 11:00 had passed on, then, of course, the sale would be void if you try to conduct a sale. The time had lapsed. They stopped the sale.

Did they do that very often?

Oh, they did that several times, I suppose at least a half dozen times in Ivanhoe. And in the meantime they were over at Willmar, all county seats, you know, Willmar and Olivia, Alexandria, you'd read about it in the paper where gangs had formed. But it's pretty much in western Minnesota. Well, I'd notify the mortgagee, you know, what had happened. Of course, they'd write a notice of postponement about that long, you know, and tell me to publish it below the original notices and publish it three more weeks, which I did. Then we would have the sale again. Well, there was several times they would come back the second time and stop the sale again. But after that went on for awhile they hardly ever came back the second time, but they would come the first time. As soon as they stopped these sales, it was all over and, of course, that got to be quite a deal. Well, there was your Holiday Association that helped the poor farmer. But I know this, that the farms and the farmers that they foreclosed around Ivanhoe, they were the type of fellows, you know, that didn't farm the way they should. The farmer's no different from a business place or anything: you tend to your business and your business will take care of you, you tend to your farm and your farm will take care of you.

What did they do to raise the farm prices?

They didn't raise them, they didn't raise them up. Floyd Olson [Governor of Minnesota], in the meantime, you know what happened there, because that was the worst part of all.

WILLIAM JOHNSON

See, I was in the Legislature in 1951. I was down there as a sergeant at arms in 1951 and I was there for four months. I had charge of the retirement room in the rear, and I was there and sat through the whole session. I talked with several of these older doormen around the state capitol and they told me. They wanted to know if I knew what the Holiday Association had done, and I said, "Yeah, I know in a general way what they had done." "Well," he said, "What they did, they came in here, they were probably 50 or 60 of them, came in here one time for the purpose of stopping the legislature in proceeding on some bills that were coming up. They were going to stop the legislature, but they went up to see Governor Olson before they did anything. So when they went up to the Governor's office and told him what they would like to do and planned to do. "Yeah," Governor Olson says, "It's all right to get a little rough." Now, can you imagine the governor of the State of Minnesota that'll yield, give in, looking for votes, there's your politics, see, looking for votes.

What kind of a man was Governor Olson?

Just that stripe, you can draw your own conclusions. A fine gentleman—he had me sit in his governor's chair one time, and I wasn't going to, but he practically forced me into the chair. I was up there on some other business. That's before all this came up and he wanted me to sit in his governor's chair, which I did. I sat in there and I said, "Damn it Floyd, no wonder you are in for office, this is a hell of a nice place to sit." Floyd was a nice guy; he smoked like the devil.

Do you think the Holiday movement had any communist infiltration in it?

Well, to me it seemed to have communist leanings at least, considering what was set up in their platform; to me it bordered on communism. I couldn't help but feel it was for something along that line; I couldn't be sure about that. But I know it wasn't anything that ever got anywhere or served any purpose, that I ever found out about.

Do you think the farmers were in real difficulties in the 1930's and they needed some help?

Oh, they weren't in half the difficulties that we were in 1890, when I came, when I was a kid.

You think the price of crops was better in the thirties than it was in the nineties?

Well, yes. In the nineties I can tell you this, my mother sold eggs in the store for 6 or 10 cents a dozen and butter for 4 or 5 cents a pound, homemade butter. And bluestem wheat was probably 35 cents a bushel, flax was 50 or 60 cents. But that was when Grover Cleveland was president.

So you don't think the farmers where in a very bad flight in the 1930's?

Well, I sort of agree they were, but I can cite you an outstanding case. We had two young men that came from Lake Wilson, Minnesota, and they came to Ivanhoe about that time. One of them bought a farm right south of town, just a half a mile out, well improved farm, a good farm, bought that. The other fellow went out west, between Ivanhoe and Hendricks, about five miles, he bought a farm out there. That fellow he stayed out there and farmed and tended to business. This fellow here, he was in town and smoking good cigars, and walking around. He didn't dissipate or anything like that, but he liked to be around town and blow; he was complaining about everything. Everything and everybody was wrong except him. It wasn't long until he lost his farm from foreclosure. This other young man went out there, and he didn't only finance the first farm, but he bought a second one. When he died, he had a half a section; this fellow lost that quarter section. And they came to Ivanhoe just exactly the same time and the two were friends and they were the same type of people. Now there's a concrete example right there. Because that one fellow, he was there on Main Street, always had a big cigar, rolled it around and told eveybody what to do, instead of being out there farming. This fellow farmed; he would tend to business. That fellow didn't. There's an example right there.

William Johnson, photo by Dan Setterberg, December 1, 1972.

Andrew Tkach, photo by Larry Jochims, April 28, 1972.

Tkach, Andrew
S176

Andrew Tkach was a Jackson County farmer who served on the Hunter Township Board. He was active in the Farm Holiday Association and served as an officer.

How strong would you say — looking back at the activities of the Farmers' Holiday and the Non-Partisan League but primarily the Farmers' Holiday — how strong was that in percentage with the number of farmers that were involved? Would you say it was fifty percent?

Yes, yes, yes it was. It was definitely very strong, very strong. In fact, I'll tell you, my brother and I went to a . . . we were delinquent, too, on interest and taxes. And the Prudential Insurance Company carried our loan and they started mortgage foreclosures on us on our home place. I was away from home at that time. I was engaged in the service of the state liquor department. When liquor came back, I was one of the investigators and I spent five years in that department.

The Prudential Insurance Company published a notice of foreclosure on our farm, on our home. I think I was in Bemidji at that time, I was away from home, so I called from either Bemidji or Detroit Lakes, I don't remember, and I told my brother that . . . well, I got already a notice from my sister . . . sent me the publication of the mortgage foreclosure notice in the *Standard*. That's supposed to be printed three different times, and that just made me feel awful because during the war, brother Jack — that's my brother, he was younger than I — was drafted in the military service to go fight an enemy overseas and here Prudential Insurance Company was advertising to sell our farm on the same courthouse lawn that my brother was drafted from into the military service with other boys. An enemy here and how about going and fighting that enemy across?

So anyway I talked to my brother when I got the notice from home that was published in the *Standard* that our place was going to be foreclosed on and I said, by golly, we've got to go see the Prudential people, because if nothing was done they'll sell you out and that's the way it would have been. But we met with . . . we made an appointment with the Prudential people and we came on a Saturday and they had their office in the Foshay Tower. My brother and I went there, so we told them who we were and what we came there for. We didn't have to tell them who we were, because they already knew, because they served notice on the place to sell it. And my dad was still living then.

The Farm Holiday, just to give you an idea of what the Farm Holiday was doing at that time . . . we mentioned to a fellow by the name of McGinnis and, oh, the other man's name, but they were the heads of Prudential Insurance, our group, the office in Minneapolis. And we told them who we were and why we came there, that we came . . . that they couldn't somehow leave us alone there on the place for another year or two and maybe the situation would change. There would be some money to pay these delinquencies. We were delinquent on our interest and taxes both. And we told them that we had our Farm Holiday in Jackson County and I was vice-chairman at that time, Charley Johnson was the main boy, and if he couldn't attend some of our meetings, I took over time and again. And anyway, we came there and told them that we had a Farm Holiday in Jackson County. McGinnis and what's the other fellow's name — I'd like to remember the name — but we told them that we had the Farm Holiday in Jackson County and if they were going to carry out the foreclosure notice and sell the place, that if they came into Jackson County there would be trouble. And so I — oh I'm trying to remember — McGinnis and Duford, a French name, and Duford and

McGinnis said, when we were visiting in the office with these two men, they said that they agreed. They seen our point. They knew why we were there, and if they came to Jackson County and if there was going to be a sheriff's sale of this place, there would be trouble.

Then just for a moment they talked to each other, just a few words, and said, "Well, we can see what this is, so call in our attorney," the attorney who was instructed to carry out the foreclosure on this farm. And they called their attorney in and told him to cancel all further publications in the *Standard*, to stop right now, no more publications foreclosing on us. And that farm is still alive today, from the action of that day. They called their attorney in and instructed him to cancel further publication of the foreclosure.

So that's the strongest the Farm Holiday was here. It was really strong ... it meant trouble for anybody that would have tried to carry out, and from my point of view — the way I felt at that time — I was tempted to kill somebody. Because my folks came there on the prairie, it was bare as the palm of your hand. There was nothing there, no buildings, no trees, no roads, no highways, no nothing. And they built it up and then have a son go down there across to fight the enemy and this one over here is going to take it from you. And when we told them that we have a Farm Holiday here, call in our attorney and instruct him not to, no further publications in the *Standard* and to this day, I think, if I was home — I haven't been home for some while because my disability keeps me in the hospital — but it would be something to see that from that time, and that was the strength of the Farm Holiday.

The other organization, the Non-Partisan League, that was coming into Minnesota from the Dakotas, but the Farm Holiday, that was really a strong militant, potent organization.

Were most of the leaders of the Farm Holiday from the old Non-Partisan League from this area?

They were, yes they were. They were from the Non-Partisan League.

How did the Farm Holiday start out then? Was it just kind of spontaneous movement or did somebody start it in some other parts of the state, then come down here?

No, no . . . Minnesota, Minnesota was about the first, because Floyd Olson declared a moratorium on all the debts. There were fights and I think some fellows even got killed during that time. It wasn't . . . it didn't get really out of hand, but he knew that that was the trouble and so he . . . he says we got to stop it . . . .

Were you very close to the Minnesota president of the Farmers' Holiday, John Bosch?

John Bosch, yes.

Then the national president was Milo Reno?

Milo Reno, yes.

You met both those people?

Yes. I think I got some correspondence where we sent some letters to him. He was in Washington. It was so bad we needed something right away.

I was up at the Minnesota Historical Society in St. Paul looking for some things on the Farmers' Holiday and they have nothing up there on the Farmers' Holiday at all.

They don't, huh?

There are just a few scattered papers in other collections. And I really think someday it would be nice to get some of the stuff like you've got — you know, correspondence with people — and have it put in a place where it can be used by somebody. Because none of the county entries even mentioned it, the Farmers' Holiday or the Non-Partisan League or any of this type of farmers' activity, and all these counties around here are primarily agricultural. They were agricultural communities when these events happened and it isn't mentioned in the county histories.

Well, this town itself, they had a law-and-order group organized and one evening we were at the town hall — there was a little town hall here — and we wanted to know. They were Farm Holiday fellows. And there were some city fellows. They thought we had no right to rough up anybody or threaten anybody, and Charley Johnson was the vice-chairman — he was the chairman of the Farm Holiday — and while we were waiting for a certain fellow to come, he never showed up. Charley Johnson says "What's the use of just waiting here, we just as well have a meeting right now." So Charley Johnson took over the meeting right then and did we have a mass meeting. We expressed our views and why we were here and all that, and golly that was just too much for the town. The town wasn't on our side. I don't know . . . the town is a Republican town here. They profit from the good programs that came through in time, whoever they're accredited to, but the town votes Republican strong and yet their bread is buttered from another source.

Did the Farmers' Holiday here get involved in the picketing or closing down the roads, stopping transportation?

Well, there was quite a feeling . . . not to deliver cream to the creamery, and that was one of the things. But that was trying to get a price. The motive was to get a price, and that was coming so slow like it would never come. And then, of course, our farm program came in.

Yes, that broke the back of it.

That really broke, too. And then, of course, the closing of the banks, and that really saved the money of a good many people who had any money yet to save. The banks had to be liquidated and had to appoint receivers to handle it, because it was only a percentage of the money returned to somebody that actually saved their money and left it in the bank. But that was that, and it was rather slow coming back . . . .
That's something that I didn't want to get to any part of it because there was this feeling, gol, anything but good.

It could have gone either way, very violent or very. . .

Yes, that's just like I'm telling you when the publication came of selling our place the sheriff's sale, the foreclosure. My brother went over there to fight and here I have an enemy. . . I'd have been tempted to kill somebody, I'll tell you that. I'm glad such a thing didn't happen. Man in his normal frame of mind, but when you're threatened, your home is threatened, you're going to get up and fight, and I guess that's what we do.

Ebeling, Louis
S452

Louis Ebeling was born in Sibley, Iowa. His family moved to Nobles County in 1913 and settled north of Rushmore, Minnesota. He started farming on his own in 1929.

Do you recall much in the way of any Farm Holiday activity in the 1930's?

Oh, yes. I know, we had a neighbor that lived right west of us—he was a good fellow, too—but he rented a farm, it was kind of a poor farm, too. He rented it from the bank here in Rushmore, and of course he couldn't pay his rent. They had a mortgage on his personal property, his horses, and machinery, so they sold him out that winter. Well, I remember, me and the neighbor that lived next to him, we went to Reading the day before the sale. Reading was hot on this Farm Holiday stuff, you know. So, I said, "If you boys ever done anything for the farmer, you better be there tomorrow." Course, I just said it in a joking way more than anything. I didn't figure that they'd be there. But they were there . . . . But, anyhow, the next day we were all at the sale and Pete Peters was the auctioneer. He jumped up on the porch and he announced the terms of the sale. Here was a fellow from Adrian—I forget what his name was—but he was the head guy of the Farm Holiday. And he says, "Before you have a sale here today, you're going to have to turn the papers over to this man, and you're going to leave him enough equipment so he can farm an eighty." He says, "You're going to leave him three horses, a plow, and a wagon." I don't know, different things like that. And, I tell you, Pete was pretty hard-boiled, you know. I tell ya, Pete, he never said a word. He talked to the clerk and the clerk jumped in the car and went to Rushmore. He went and got the papers, and turned the papers over, and they left him so much stuff to farm with when they had the sale. And then, later on, north of Wilmont, there was a man name of Torkelson. They sold him out, and, I don't know, he was hooked up with the Federal Reserve in Minneapolis. Anyhow, that big shot was there from Minneapolis, the clerk in the sale. And, of course, the Farm Holiday, they got rough, and they started roughing him up. He got out of there, I'll tell ya.

Right at the sale?

Yes, sir.

They never held that sale?

They never had that sale that day, but they had it about two, three weeks later. They made a settlement with him, so they had it then.

Did he have some protection there? The second time?

I don't know, I didn't go to the sale the second time. But later on, after I moved to Bigelow, why I was in the store there one day, and this Torkelson he had moved from Bigelow, see, up there north of Wilmont. In fact, he lived in the same section with us there, north of Wilmont. So after we moved to Bigelow, I was in the store there one day, and the fellow working there in the store, a fellow by the name of Matt Waltersdorf, he says, "Say, you didn't happen to know a fellow up there by the name of Chris Torkelson?"

I said, "Ya, I did." I says, "I lived neighbor to him."

Then he says, "You know, I worked in the bank here," he says, "and he come from here and the bank here had mortgage on his stuff. Of course the bank went closed, and a bank in Minneapolis took over, and they was going to have a sale, and," he says, "he come back here and he calls Minneapolis and says, 'Say, you boys, if you fellows want to sell this guy out, you better come here yourselves and clerk the sale,' he says, 'I come just darn near getting strung up in one of them big cottonwood trees'." And, I'll tell ya, that's just the way it was, too.

So, Nobles County knew about the Torkelsons?

Yes, sir.

Those farmers were pretty angry, huh?

They were, yah. Of course, I'll tell ya, the bank probably wasn't to blame. They had their money in it. It was just one of them deals—why the Bigelow bank went closed, you see, so they had to sell all them guys out.

Who did you, and other farmers, blame? How did you try to make sense of this situation?

By, gosh, I don't know who we blamed, really.

Not your banker? Insurance companies, did they foreclose?

Well, yes, a lot of it was, you know. Here they had bought and during the first World War, you know, land went up just like it did now. It went from, you might say, sixty to seventy dollars an acre to three hundred and fifty dollars.

That's quite a jump, from sixty or seventy dollars to three hundred and fifty an acre.

That's right, and then, you know, when the depression come, it just kept going down. Well, most of them fellas, they probably had ten thousand in a forty thousand dollar farm, and they just couldn't make it.

What happened to those people that lost farms during the depression?

Well, I'll tell you. A lot of them started in again. If they weren't too old, most of them overcome it. But if they were, say, fifty years old or older, why they really never got back on their feet.

THE CROWD THAT HALTED THE EXECUTION SALE

Farmers' Holiday Association protesters, Granite Falls, January, 1933. Granite Falls *Tribune,* February 2, 1933.

Tatge, Orville
S215

Orville Tatge was born in South Dakota and moved to Benson in 1927. He was president of the Swift County NFO in 1963. He also served as DFL county treasurer in 1969. Mr. Tatge was a farmer.

Let's start out with some background on you and your family. You were born in this area?

I actually was born in South Dakota, north of Sioux Falls, but I moved here at the age of seven. I really consider myself a Minnesotan. My mother and father had lived in this area and moved in 1918. And then in '27 we moved here again, and I was seven years old at that time.

So you got to see and live through the depression?

Yes, I was here during the bank crash. I remember the banks closing, the depression and the drought years here.

Your father was an auctioneer you said?

Yes, my father auctioneered in probably three or four counties. I remember in the spring and the fall, when farm sales were being held; why there would be six sales a week, a sale every day.

Were those farm sales at all related to the Farmers' Holiday Movement?

Oh yes, there was some of that. There were probably a lot of farm sales that were stopped by the Farmers' Holiday Movement. Some of them were stopped before they ever became advertised and the like, and there were a few stopped after they were advertised. I remember Farm Holiday members going and buying. They just all got together and were the only bidders at a sale and they bought the stuff for little or nothing, and they gave it back to the farmers. And of course, in this case the bank was the loser. But I don't ever remember the Farm Holiday actually stopping a sale that my dad had, but I heard of them stopping other sales.

The Farmers' Holiday Movement was a strong movement here in the area?

Yes, it was quite strong. I can think of quite a few of the prominent fellows at that time that were in the Farm Holiday Movement. I would say that Swift County probably had as strong a Farm Holiday Movement as most any county in the state.

And your family lived on a farm, were farmers?

We lived on a farm all the time, yes. We lived on ... well we rented farms until 1937, so you go back to those years. My wife can bear this out, in Dakota, too, that on March 1st the roads were just full of hay racks and horses with moving furniture and the likes. Actually, it was a kind of a thrill to the kids to get to move.... We bought one farm from Aetna Life Insurance Company, and they made the deal so attractive you couldn't hardly turn it down. And this was how fair they were about it. They really didn't want the land. Now I think a lot of people would want the land, but at that time they didn't want the land. Really what they wanted was to have their money invested and get three-and-a-half, four percent interest—was a good interest rate at that time.

Things have sure changed today. Going back to your father as an auctioneer and the Farmers' Holiday Movement, what really was the Farmers' Holiday Movement?

Well, of course the Farmers' Holiday Movement was basically organized to help the farmer get a better income and better living conditions as a result of it. But their part in farm sales was to try and forestall the foreclosing of bankers on farmers, so the farmer could get a total and save his farming operation. And this was good for the farmer that had a fighting chance. But there were some cases where the farmer had already skipped out, gone to the city and found a job, and was just waiting for the family to get rid of the stuff and move in and follow him. . . .I remember seeing the Farm Holiday sale. But my dad's reasoning with these people was that the man wasn't there, the livestock wasn't half being taken care of, why stop the sale? Now when the man was there and then my dad was all for it. And I'm sure he chipped in money. And they'd take up a collection and they'd buy the stuff and turn it back to the farmer. And the bank had to take for it, because there was nobody else to bid against them, and the bank had foreclosed on this, so they had to take whatever it brought.

So the Farmers' Holiday Association, then . . . going to these sales was just one part of its program?

Yes, that was one part of it. They went to the legislature, I think they had lobbyists, and they were trying to get better prices and the likes. I think they were probably, basically, the real active arm of the Farmers Union. The Farmers Union, as we think of it today, is more a business, and these were the people who were active to get a better price for farmers. Farmers Union Grain Terminal Association today wants to buy the grain as cheap as they can. They want to make a profit on it. They want to show a margin where these people were out to really try and do something for the farmer out there. They didn't care if it was Farmers Union or what it was, but they wanted a better price. And they wanted to stop anything, any foreclosure or anything like that they could until this farmer could get a better price and hang on.

Were there any other big farmers' association groups?

Oh, of course. I think probably Farm Bureau was the first one. And my dad was a member of Farm Bureau at one time, but Farm Bureau has never been anything but a service organization. Oh, I shouldn't say that. In this area probably. Out in California the Farm Bureau has a bargaining group that bargains for the price of tomatoes, for the price of lettuce and radishes and things like this, but they don't want to take hold of the thing, all of the agriculture, and do it. Really Farm Bureau's big thing is service. They want to sell feed back and make a profit on it and they wanted to sell insurance, and I've heard this argued, but in spite of their arguments, the biggest membership of Farm Bureau of any county in the United States is in Cook County, Illinois and Cook County, Illinois has just a handful of farms. But they have a lot of members there who pay in and get cheaper insurance and things like this. So Farm Bureau has typically been this kind of an organization, a service organization. Farmers Union turned out this way. I don't think they were intended that way when they were started, but this is the way they turned out.

How did more radical farmers' organizations grow out of either of these two organizations? Was there any sort of set issue that . . . ?

Your Farmers' Holiday is probably considered the most radical farm organization there ever was, but I don't call it too radical. What they wanted to do was help save the farmer and help keep him on the farm, and what other means was there to do if they were being sold out and through no fault of their own they couldn't make their payments? It's basically crop failure or prices were so low that . . . I'll give you an example. We rented this farm from the state of Minnesota for five dollars an acre, which was considered fair cash rent. In 1932 we had a terrific crop and we had sixty bushels of oats to the acre, real good quality oats, worth eight cents a bushel. And eight cents a bushel at sixty bushels to the acre is $4.80. And we owed the state of Minnesota five dollars an acre rent and that didn't give us anything to live on or pay our expenses and the likes. And this is an example of the conditions. And while the state of Minnesota . . . we told them what it was, take the whole crop, and write the five dollars an acre off. And they said no, they would honor a third of it. If we would deliver a third of the crop, why then they'd consider our rent paid. And this was fair. It left us very little to live on, in spite of it.

But better than had you given it all away.

Yes, rather than having to give it all away and still owe twenty cents an acre rent.

And you said that there were a lot of renters at this time, so this was the condition for a lot of the people here?

Oh yes, I saw some tough times, but there was a lot of people that had tougher times than we did. My dad was an auctioneer, and this helped out. This was a supplement to the income. We, in the early thirties, started a milk route and this helped. We got a little more for our milk delivering. We used to raise tomatoes and carrots and onions and radishes and deliver them in town, melons and the like. One summer we sold two hundred dollars worth of tomatoes alone, which was a big thing at that time. Two hundred dollars today doesn't sound like much. But at that time it was a big thing. . . .

Oh yes, Floyd Olson was supported real well I thought, and I think he was accepted pretty well. And then Elmer Benson. When Floyd died, Elmer Benson took over, and Elmer was supported real good too first time he ran. He wasn't supported very well at all the second time. I've never quite figured that out. I suppose there was a reason. I think I mentioned to you about the fact that Elmer had accumulated a lot of land and stuff and there was people jealous of him and thought maybe that this wasn't the thing to do. But I think Elmer wasn't a rich man when he got to be governor, probably wasn't wealthy at all. But he happened to be in a position to know some people that could help him a little bit, and if you could come up with anywheres from two to five hundred dollars, why you could help him out a little, and he had the nerve. Actually, at the time a lot of people thought he was foolish, and when it worked out well then they thought he was hoggish. But I don't blame him at all. I think probably I'd have done the same thing, and I don't see anything wrong about what he did. And he ended up being a fairly wealthy man.

Didn't you say too he got most of his land from the insurance companies, not from the farmer?

Right. He didn't take from the farmer; he'd pick up land that the people, insurance company or the mortgage company had foreclosed on and the farmer was already out of the picture. And then he picked it up. I don't think he . . . well he didn't have money to loan out on farms, so he couldn't foreclose on them. I mean he just picked them up. My dad bought two farms the same way. We just had, well, two hundred and forty acre farm and we had to make a three hundred dollar downpayment in July and two hundred dollars the following first of March. And we had the farm. I think it was three-and-a-half percent interest, and that was bought from Aetna Life Insurance Company. State of Minnesota, I believe we paid — that wasn't as big a farm, and I think we paid about four hundred dollars, four hundred and some dollars down on that, and I think that was four percent interest. One farm was thirty-seven dollars an acre and the other was forty-three. It was merely that Elmer Benson had access to people who could help him out a little more and he had the nerve to do it and it worked out. But he did get to be a controversial figure because of this.

Mattson, Axel
S221

Axel Mattson was born on March 29, 1886 in Cokato, Wright County. He lived there for twenty years. After teaching country school in North Dakota for two years, he went to Minneapolis. He began farming in Goodhue County in 1920 and stayed there until 1933 when he moved to Buffalo, Minnesota and began doing highway maintenance work.

O.K., going back to Montevideo and the thirties, how did you get involved in the Farm Holdiay?

Well, I'll tell you. I was always at that end of society, at the left side. I always favored the cooperatives. I was very much interested in Floyd Olson. He was a good man. I helped organize cooperatives. I helped organize a cooperative funeral association, shipping association, cooperative store at Montevideo. They all went down. I did organize three credit unions with the one we had in Montevideo. You know, when you did something like that, they recognized you by issuing you a founder's button. And that credit union in Montevideo is doing very well. I think they got between three and four hundred thousand dollars. I'm not sure because I haven't been in touch with them lately.

Did you take part in any of the penny auctions that the Farm Holiday had?

No.

Were there any up around Montevideo that you can remember?

Well, I don't recall that there were any penny auctions. But I know there was resistance, real resistance. These people that tried to ship livestock down to South St. Paul, we resisted them. I didn't take any physical action, but some of the boys over there did, and they kept quite a bit of livestock from going to South St. Paul. It was terrible. I had to have an auction when I quit farming in '33. I had a nice sow with four or five pigs. I got seven dollars for the whole bunch. I got thirteen cents a bushel for corn. And oats, you could hardly give away. And my livestock went for twenty-five dollars a piece for the cows. The machinery, I had good machinery. It went for practically nothing. I had the auction in February, 1933.

Was it the depression that forced you to quit farming?

Yes.

Yes, it was in the depression I quit farming. That's right.

You couldn't make a go of it?

Well, I'll tell you. I tried to rent a farm after I moved off the home farm, and in order to rent a farm, you had to pay the rent in advance. Otherwise, they wouldn't rent to you. So I thought to myself, I'd better not get into that. I suppose I could have found a farm. But you know, at that time the renter had no chance. So we bought a little place in Buffalo and I got a job with the state.

Were there a lot of farm foreclosures, mortgage foreclosures?

Oh, yes, there was some. There was some alright.

A lot around Montevideo?

Well, I don't think there was so many there.

But still the farmers reacted against it; you said that they were . . .

Oh, it was just terrible. You couldn't sell anything and get any money for it. You ship some livestock down to South St. Paul and you'd get two or three dollars for it. What in the world, you couldn't live that way. Look now, holy Moses! Did you know we could get along when hogs were seven cents a pound? We got along. We made a living.

Did you take part in any demonstrations?

Well, not too much.

Just a little lip service.

We were roaming around, you know, a bunch of us, nights, to watch how things were going. I know one night we went down to St. Paul to consult with Floyd Olson. I was along there.

On that march on the capitol—was this the march on the capitol?

No.

Wasn't that when the farmers went up there to picket at the capitol in March of 1933?

Oh, yes, we went to the capitol. They picketed a lot at the South St. Paul livestock houses too. You know, that's where they butcher the cattle.

Did you go along?

No.

No? What was this time you were talking about when you took part? What time was this? You said as far as demonstrations...

I'll tell you we went down to St. Paul one night to consult

with Floyd Olson. Three, four farmers that were interested in the thing.

Did you talk to him?

Well, we all did, yes.

Personally?

Oh, Floyd Olson was a wonderful man. You know, it's funny with people—a man like him, he had the good will of everybody. He was a wonderful man. You know, the boys down at Austin, where Hormel has a slaughterhouse, they went on strike once when Floyd Olson was governor. And they wouldn't let Hormel get into the freezing plant or into the plant at all. So Hormel went to work and asked Floyd Olson to come over. And Floyd Olson went there and he went to the union and he said, "You boys better go over and fix things up at the slaughterhouse." The boys went over there and opened up, got together with Hormel and they've been a pretty solid union ever since.

Did you have any contact with John Bosch?

John Bosch?

Yes.

Oh, I knew him.

Personally?

Oh, yes. We went, oh, to. . .

Washington, D.C. didn't you?

Where in the world was it we went?

Washington, D.C.

No, we went there, too, that was in '33. We went there to talk to our Congressman.

About the farmers' situation?

Yes. I was on the State Board of the Educational Organization of Farmers Union at that time. So I went with the State Farmers Union Organization in Washington. I don't know if it did any good.

What did you think of John Bosch?

Well, I thought he was a little bit to the left. A little more than I was. But he was pretty capable. We went with him to a town and I can't recall what town it was. We spent the whole day there. John Bosch had some good ideas. But, you know, you can't go to the left beyond a certain place. Otherwise, you run against the customs and the wishes of the society.

You thought John Bosch went too far to the left?

Well, I though he was pretty far over.

Did you know Milo Reno? He was the national president of the Farm Holiday?

Oh, yes.

Did you know him?

Not personally.
I didn't know him.

How did you meet Harry Haugland? How did you meet him and what did you think of him? Harry Haugland?

Well, I'll tell you. You know, I always promoted the cooperative. That's to the left, a certain amount, but not too far. And Harry Haugland, he was pretty far to the left with his ideas.

That's what I thought of him. I tell you, as early as 1930, in there some year, there was a guy who came as a complete stranger. I was connected with the **Farmers Union Education Organization**. And, he came over there and tried to use his influence with the things, at this time, we called communist propaganda. And right away, I abhorred his idea. I couldn't endorse him at all. But those things happen and I know that he was a communist.

Well, what did Harry Haugland do in Montevideo? I mean, what part did he play?

Some of these far left fellows tried out commune farming. Farm together, and divide it at the end. That didn't work. Harry took part in every public anti-demonstration.

Demonstration of every sort?

Yes, every demonstration. And I, as far as I was concerned, I didn't like the way Haugland did it.

Did you think that the Farmers' Holiday was effective, their movement?

Well, I think they had to do it. We had lost a lot. At that time, there was no recourse or resource for the farmer. What could he do? He couldn't sell. He could raise crops, but he couldn't sell them. He couldn't sell livestock. What was he going to do? He was at the end of the rope.

Do you think Roosevelt did a lot for the farmer?

Yes, that's my opinion. Many people didn't believe that. But I think he was one of the greatest men and the greatest friend that the common people had. And you know we had the Tennessee Valley Authority and that was the first wonderful

AXEL MATTSON

thing that they did. And then we lived out in the country. If we wanted electricity, we paid about $200 a mile from the output or the source in order for the company to build a line out. In the '30's, when the President instituted the REA, that was the most wonderful thing for the farmers that ever happened. I think Roosevelt was a great President, a wonderful man.

Farmers' Holiday demonstration in St. Paul, March 22, 1933. Photo from Echo *Enterprise*.

Farmers' Holiday demonstration in St. Paul, March 22, 1933. Photo courtesy Minnesota State Historical Society.

Engebretson, John
S449

John was born in Rock County, the son of Norwegian immigrants. He was a school teacher, a farmer, and he also served as manager of the Kenneth Farmers' Elevator.

What kind of a relationship did you have with a lot of the farmers during the twenties when the Non-Partisan League was fairly active?

Well, I think we had very few farmers that belonged to it. Then when the Holiday came, we read in the paper and we heard about how they were trying to foreclose on different farms. Even with personal property, they had to try to have a share of it. Those fellows got out in force and stopped those sales. I don't think there was any sales going on. I had a little experience with the Holiday. We had a couple of fellows. One fellow... They got this idea that they should have a reduction in their debt, in their notes. All we asked them to do was to come in and fix up their notes so they wouldn't be past due. We wanted that, and if possible pay the interest. If they couldn't pay the interest, we'd ride along with them. Well, there was two fellows that wanted to have a reduction before ... and that we should cut the principle before they'd .... They had that idea. So one day I saw a car drive in, this comes out of Nobles County. Five men was in it. I knew right away this was a Holiday bunch. I know some of them belonged to the Holiday....

Two fellows came into the bank and the other fellows didn't come in. We went into the back room. They asked me, "What's the trouble between you and this customer of ours?" "Well," I says, "I don't know if there's really any trouble." I says, "We've asked him to come in and fix up his notes and renew them. If he can pay the interest, we'd like to have that or pay on the principle if he can. But, if not, we'll renew it."

"Well," they said, "Can't see anything really wrong in that."

You were being as fair as you could be.

Yes.

Trying to give him all the benefit of the doubt also.

"We'll ride along with him," I says, "If he'll just do that. But we should have that."

And they thought, "That doesn't seem unreasonable." Then they went out and they talked it over. In a day or two, they came in and fixed up, and everything was lovely. They had a man in Luverne here, Andrew Jenson was his name. I don't know what they called him, but he was the fellow that they complained to. I got a letter from him one time. He said I should come down and see him. I did. He had another fella. He wanted to know what the trouble was. "As far as I know, there's no trouble," I said. "Except that I want him to fix up the note." They were past due and I wanted to put them in order. I talked to him. I knew him real well too. I don't think that made a difference.

"Well," he says, "there's nothing wrong with that is it?" I didn't want to force him out. No clothes on him or anything. He wrote the letter to him. This fellow came in and fixed up. That's my experience with the Holiday.

You never had any sales then through your bank?
No.

JOHN ENGEBRETSON

Most of the notes you held were not real estate loans?

Most of them were on cattle.

Cattle, that was more or less on their livestock or machinery or . . .

Livestock, machinery, and stuff like that. I don't think I ever foreclosed anything. I never had a foreclosure.

Most of the time you tried to work it out?

Yes. We had some that we asked to sell, but I don't think we ever had . . . I can't remember.

Never had to really kind of get down and be nasty about the whole thing.

No, not the legal.

Yes, that can end up being kind of messy for everybody involved.

No, we never had any. Our stockholders got a dividend every year, except for two years. One time when we built a building, and another time when the times were so blame tough that we could have paid it, but it didn't look right to pay it. So I said to the board of directors, "Let's not pay any dividends now." Otherwise they got dividends right along. Finally in '47, I liquidated the whole thing. They had another new bank started. We turned the stuff over to them.

How active was the Farm Holiday around Kenneth?

Not too bad there.

It wasn't? It wasn't very well organized?

It wasn't anything. There was a lot of them there that didn't believe in it at all. I think the majority.

What were the most of them in? Were they Farm Union people or Farm Bureau people?

They were Farm Bureau people. . . .There was, once in a while, here and there one.

Oh, Yes. Well, there's always a few in every crowd. Most of the farmers were pretty prosperous up until that point. I mean, they were pretty well established in general.

Well, in a way, they were getting along all right. Nothing like today.

Yes.

There's no comparison. They got along pretty good. We had a lot of good luck starting out young fellows. They used to have a little money and got a little help from home maybe. We'd loan them a thousand, fifteen hundred dollars or something; two thousand dollars, to buy stuff with and get started farming. We had very little trouble. Most of the fellows made it. They were honest, and it was okay.

David E. Olson
S444

David Olson was born and raised on the farm where he presently lives. His parents are Swedish immigrants. He is a farmer who attended country school through grade 8.

In the thirties things got pretty tough, didn't they?

Yes, it really come to a standstill. It wasn't... prices... well, it wasn't worth hauling to town.

Where did you usually haul crops from here?

Oh, we used to haul to Mountain Lake, Trimont— haul with horses sleds in the winter, wagons in the fall. Made one trip a day. Of course, we always had livestock too. There was quite a lot of grain to haul, too.

When do you remember the first time that farmers kind of got together in the thirties to do something about that problem?

Well, I can't give you any particular dates. It kind of just grew. It got worse and worse and they wondered what they were going to do. They used to get together and discuss their problems and they didn't know what they were going to do. And then, of course, in order to get some attention, why we just got organized; we tried to stop the sales. A lot of farmers were being sold out. Then they got together.

Would these be renters that were being sold out?

Well, I suppose it would have been mostly renters. Of course, there were a lot of others too that even owned their farms who were really getting into difficulty. You couldn't get money to pay the taxes. So they got together. When they had these sales, of course, why, they just decided they'd pay a few pennies and that was it. If anybody started to bid too much, why they just tapped them a little bit on the shoulder and that was it.

What if a guy still went ahead and bid even after he tapped him on the shoulder?

He didn't.

That was it.

There was such a crowd there when they had a sale that they had to carry a few ropes and a few clubs— sort of an idea of what might happen. And I think it would have happened if they would have continued it.

You think it was that tense, huh?

It was tense.

Now this would be household sales?

Oh, farm sale, livestock and machinery.

So anything went for a few pennies?

Everything went for a few pennies and, of course, when dusk started up, the sale was called off. But, you see, when it was advertised they had to go through with it. The banker, of course, he wanted to call it off but he couldn't. You see, that was the law. It was legally called and that was it. But it didn't take long before they didn't call any sales.

What happened to this stuff that these other farmers bought for pennies?

Oh, they just returned it to the fellow you see, right there.

Now John Bosch tells that sometimes he made arrangements with sheriffs in some counties that they could go ahead and call the Governor, who was Floyd Olson, and they could get permission from the Governor not to have the sale. Did that ever happen in Jackson County?

Well, yes. They had the intent that if you assured a sale there, you had to be on the courthouse steps. But, of course, the sheriff, he just couldn't stay on the steps. He had the crowd from behind, so he was soon forced off the steps and then he couldn't hold a sale.

Those sales, were there lots of people with ropes and clubs too, to get the idea across?

They were around.

Now you were saying, before, when we were talking out here for a moment, that there weren't any specific leaders in the county, but the farmers just sort of all came together.

Yes. Of course, there was always some that was a little bit more in the forefront but I can't remember. George, my brother, of course, he was pretty active in here; talked to people. And this Charlie Johnson, he was active in it. But I never really had too much to do with him. But he was around.

But you were saying the farmers all felt a sort of common sense of desperation.

Yes. There wasn't really anybody that objected. When we asked elevators and creameries to close up ... I, my brother, and a couple other fellows, I can't recall their names, we just went around and saw the managers and asked them to close up and that was all. They did. They didn't want us to get upset.

Did the farmers generally cooperate with this? They wouldn't try to sneak in and sell . . .

No, not after they closed up. There wasn't much opposition. Nobody really seemed to oppose it much. Pretty general opinion that it was all right.

So you had the whole county pretty well closed up?

Yes, it was three, four days that there wasn't anything moving out of Jackson County.

Why didn't the farmers really revolt? Why wasn't there more violence, do you think?

Well, of course, nobody wants violence. There was no violence here in Jackson County. Of course, in Iowa there was problems. But we never had any of that here.

Do you think it's mainly because the farmers didn't want to get into that or did they feel not that desperate?

It really doesn't do any good anyway. If you could call attention to government and such, that was about the idea of it.

But you think if somebody at one of these sales would have tried to push too hard, there might have been a little shoving and banging of heads.

Well, it could have been but it never was here. They took the hint and that was it.

So there weren't many farmers in opposition to it locally?

No, not that I know of around here. Most of them around here seemed to have been in favor of it.

How did the sheriff and county attorney react to all this at the time?

Well, the sheriff seemed to be pretty sympathetic too. He didn't . . .

Do you think the county attorney was pretty sympathetic too?

Well, I don't know if he was ever involved in any case here. It never got that far so that he got involved in it.

Now did any specific insurance companies, that you remember, try to foreclose farms around here?

No, there was some foreclosed but I couldn't say who they were. I know one insurance company; they always painted their buildings the same colors. You could tell, you know, when they . . .

Buy the same color and paint all the buildings that color.

Yes, that's about it.

Did you know quite a few farmers that lost their land during the thirties?

No. You see, that mortgage moratorium come on here pretty fast. That kind of took care of it until it straightened out.

Do you think that the pressure that you farmers put on it was responsible in getting that moratorium law passed?

Oh, I think so. I'm sure it did.

You think the governor and the legislature realized that the farmers were in a state of revolt almost?

Yes, I think so.

Do you think this is one of the really hotbeds of all that upset and demonstrations, in Jackson here?

Well, I don't know if it was any other county that closed the creameries and elevators up. It was really quite strong in here.

Did you go to St. Paul when a lot of farmers marched on the capitol?

No, I was never up there. My brother, George, was up there.

Did he think the governor treated them pretty well when they got up there?

I never heard him say anything about that.

At least he addressed the farmers; that was a helpful thing.

Yes, Floyd Olson was pretty sympathetic. He understood what was involved. Otherwise we would never have had these laws passed.

Why do you think he was so sympathetic?

Well, why shouldn't he be? When the country comes to a standstill you have to become sympathetic, whether you want to or not.

Sure. Was it something in his own background that would have made him understand?

I would say so. He came up the hard way. He was a hard worker— lumberjack, I think he'd been. I have a book on that period, when he campaigned, so I know pretty well what he was thinking.

Do you think he was a good governor?

I figure he was a good governor for that day and age.

Some people think he might even had become president had he lived.

He would have, I think. If he had lived, I think he would have.

Did he have strong support around here?

Oh, yes. I remember when he was in the state of Minnesota, Franklin D. Roosevelt was here at that time, and he rode with him. He said, "I wish I had you in Washington instead of the state of Minnesota." He thought very favorably of him.

That worked to your advantage too, didn't it? To have a governor who was such a good friend of the President at that time?

I think so. They understood the problem and you see we got these farm programs through, where we got this price support, you know. I had corn setting here that wasn't worth anything. Then he got that program through where you got a loan of forty-five cents a bushel. And the resale program came along. I eventually sold that corn for over a dollar a bushel.

What was it before that? Less than a dime a bushel?

Oh, yes, it was less; five, six cents. Well, in fact, there was no market for it. You couldn't pay the freight.

You think that was one of the best pieces of legislation that Roosevelt and the governor passed, the price supports?

Well, it certainly put the farmers on their feet again. I remember we had a fellow came out to here from Chicago; he was a union carpenter. But, of course, everything closed up in the cities and he came out here looking for work. He has some relative here. But there wasn't anything for him to do here. He got a place to live and we used to get in little debates. He was a stong union man and he always said he had to get labor back to work. He said then that this thing would take care of itself, and we always said that the farm economy is the base of this country. If they got the farmers' income back up, you fellows will be taken care of automatically. He never believed that. But then when we got this corn price supports through, right away in this country here, in this here ceiling program, the building started right here.

Right here on the farm.

Right here on this farm. From then on he had so much work he didn't know what to do with it. I built this big black storage tank out here to seal the corn, and that corn crib out there. Everything started moving again when we got these loans through. Then I used to remind him; I says, "Now you see what happens when the farmers get a little money in their pocket; the economy picks right up."

Did he believe you then?

Well, he had to believe me.

How many people moved out from the city back onto the farm?

Well, there weren't so many that moved in here. But I remember him very well. He was a very good carpenter and, of course, everything came to a standstill in the cities. So he was trying to live wherever he could. I remember I was up to Minneapolis one time, that depression. A fellow took me around. We went down Hennepin Avenue and he said, "Well, let's turn in here." There was a great big hall there just full of people waiting to get a bowl of soup. We walked around just to look. "And this is just one place," he said, "Let's walk down a few blocks further and we'll see another one the same way." No work. They were ladling out a little soup to them. So it was a very tense time for people in the cities too.

DAVID OLSON

Did farmers out in this area tend to help take care of some of the people in the communities that were out of work? Did you supply food for them? Did most people have jobs in these little towns?

No, there wasn't much they could do about that. Everybody had to try take care of themselves. That was about it. I can't recall that anything better went on here.

They called them socialists, communists. But they didn't talk that way about the Holiday people, huh?

Well, of course, we had this here, Mrs. Birnie; you've probably heard about her. She come in here later.

Mrs. Birnie?

Yes. She came in here; had some meetings, tried to accuse the Farmers Union and Holiday movement as being organized by the communists. She said there had been communist influence in here and, of course, it was nothing but nonsense. It was just spontaneous. There wasn't outside organizers in here, why I would say at all. Unless you call John Bosch. He was around the state. I don't think you would call him a communist.

Did you ever have Milo Reno come up here at anytime?

No, I can't say . . . he was up in Minnesota. That would have been in the Farmers Union.

He was the head of the Farmers' Holiday too.

Well, I guess he was in Iowa.

But Bosch was around here quite a lot then?

Yes, he was a good organizer. He had a lot to do with it, you know, more so than anybody.

Was he a pretty good speaker?

Oh, he was terrific.

What were his strong points? Just that he knew how to move a crowd or . . .

Of course he realized what was happening. He figured something had to be done about it.

Was he a pretty good thinker? You could tell that the way he talked?

I would say he was, yes. He was pretty sound.

He's still pretty sound. We've had him on our college campus and he's spoken to a class or so.

John has got a lot of brains.

We thought sometime it would be great to have a big state time and all of you people who were involved in that all get together again.

Well, they have had sort of a reunion on the Bosch farm up there. I think they have one every year.

Have you ever gone up for that?

No, I've never gone up there.

I bet you'd find some people you knew.

Oh, I think I would.

I met Mrs. Charlie Johnson the other day. He's been gone for a long time. She's still living in Worthington.

She's still living in Worthington.

She had just thrown away a bunch of pictures from the period and I really was kind of sad by that, because I wanted to get hold of some of them.

Charlie was involved in this Non-Partisan League movement.

Oh, he was?

They darn near hung him down here one time.

Is that right!

I think they probably would have killed him if he hadn't gotten out the back door.

On the Non-Partisan League?

Yes, it was real rough.

She referred to that period and said she didn't like those politics very much and that's probably why. If he had some close calls she wouldn't like that time.

Oh, yes. He had some rough times.

You think it really saved a lot of these farms around here?

I think it did.

Were you ever in danger of losing your own farm?

Well, it was getting plenty rough, you know. We had a hard time to get the tax money together.

But you never did have anybody threaten you with taking the land for taxes?

No, no.

Did you have a mortgage on it at that time?

No, we didn't have a mortgage. It was an estate at that time. My father had died.

But you still had to meet the taxes?

Oh, we had to meet the taxes.

What happened when these people lost their farms? Where did they go?

Well, I don't know really what happened to them. I suppose some of them had to go on welfare or something.

Did a lot of them stay around here or did they move away?

Oh, some moved away, I suppose. It's really hard to recall. I can't really say what happened to some of them. It seemed like, probably, after the insurance company took over, why they still stayed on the farm and rented it.

From the insurance company?

From the insurance company.

So many of them just stayed on there and just became renters instead of owners?

Yes, then they had these here debt adjustment committees. I was on that for a time.

What did you do?

Well, I'll tell you, you see, some of them had got in kind of bad with the landlord and the debts got bigger and bigger. Some of the landlords, of course, were fairly heeled. If we could scale the debt down a little bit sometimes, why they could stay on the farm, and keep on a-going.

So you were a mediator between the man that was in trouble and the landlord?

Sort of, yes. We looked at the facts, you know . . . . We had these debt adjustment committees. They were appointed by the governor. Sometimes we could do some good and then, of course, some fellows tried to chisel out other reasonable debt too. Some of them will do that.

So it worked both ways.

It went both ways. We found that we just wouldn't go along with that.

How did you happen to be appointed by the Governor to one of these? He knew about you and your activity?

Well, I suppose he probably did.

How long did you serve on that?

Well, it was a couple, three years. From then on, of course, the things got better, so they just disappeared.

Did you ever have any difficulties in settling one of these? Did anybody ever get irate with you?

No, not really. When you get right down to talk turkey to them, why most of them were pretty reasonable.

Even the more wealthy landowners would compromise a little bit on those and scale them down?

Yes. If we seen that a tenant or someone was trying to get away with something that he shouldn't, why we'd back the landlord too.

How many were on there; two or three on each committee?

I think there was about three of us; two, three of us on the committee.

All of you were farmers?

Yes.

Well, I think most of you who were really involved in that agree that Farm Holiday was a very important factor for saving farms.

Yes, it was. No question about it. It called the government's attention to the conditions...well, it was getting quite serious you know. When it gets so bad you can't get a-hold of a penny, why you begin to wonder what's going to happen.

Lund, Clarence
S450

Clarence Lund was born and raised on the farm his grandmother homesteaded in 1864. He farmed there until his recent retirement. Clarence graduated from Augsburg College with a masters in mathematics and English and a minor in biology. He was a high school instructor, a weatherman, a bookkeeper; he then returned to farming for 25 years, now retired.

How did you see John Bosch? Was he an effective organizer, an effective leader?

Well, yes, I think he was. He gave everything that he had to the organization.

Was he a good speaker?

Yes, he developed to be a good speaker. He started out as a farmer out in this community. He did a lot of reading. He always had a lot of books, and always took interest in economic problems locally, state and nationally. Even the younger generation are still doing that.

What was Richard's [contribution] to the organization?

Probably, not so much like John Bosch. But he did go out to meetings and attended all meetings within this area. I don't recall that he did any speaking, but I suppose he did.

John did most of it?

Yes.

What about the other brothers? Did Earl or....

Earl and Herbert were active on stopping trucks. There's

where they worked. Herbert got thrown into jail at Anoka, I think it was.

What was he thrown into jail for?

Well, blocking traffic and I suppose he was the leader. They had to bail him out. I recall that.

What ever happened to the charges? Were they ever processed?

I think they dropped it. And oh, another thing here in the Lake Lillian area, we had a man by the name of Stocklan. He farmed about six or seven miles east of here; a great big man. So when they had a sale foreclosure, then the Farm Holiday would have this man at the sheriff's door. He was a great big man. He covered pretty near the whole door. When they were going to start the sale, then Sheriff Anderson would point to that man.

This would be Paul Anderson?

Yes, Paul Anderson. I suppose he was sympathetic with the group. But he'd point to that man, how could he get by? That was it.

Did that postpone sales or a lot of times did that put them off entirely?

It put them off, I think most of them entirely. As far as I know, entirely.

Did you ever go to any of these foreclosures?

No, I never did.

Did you say to us that you went to the capitol once?

Yes. But that was later. That was in . . . must have been in '33.

The Holiday was one of the groups that promoted it?

Yes, that promoted it. It seemed to me that it was Governor Benson that set in the administration. It must have been.

Well, it's about that same time.

I'm pretty sure that it was Governor Benson. Because on the adult education program, some of the men would go in and see the governor. I think one by the name of Nels Nelson. I don't recall where he was from. He could go in to see the governor if he wanted to. Something like Severeid, a great newsman. He could see Governor Olson when he was a student at the University of Minnesota.

What did you do when you got up there?

Oh, I didn't do anything in particular. I was in the corridor there and watched the people move around. *The Minneapolis Star* took a picture of the group and Clinton Haroldson, you can see him. I know my back is toward the picture. I clipped it out as a reminder that I was there, but I lost it afterwards.

Was the idea, then, just to show mass support for the farm problem?

Yes. . . .

So between selling memberships and then later going up there, were there any other activities locally that you were involved in?

No, I was a member of the Farmers Union all the time and also the action group till a year ago. I'm not active that way anymore.

Do you think during the period of time that the Holiday was so active, that times were pretty desperate for farmers?

Yes.

Do you think the farmers were about ready to revolt if something wouldn't have been done for them?

They were pretty close to that. The way I look at it, they were real poor. Many farmers that didn't have too big a mortgage were in difficulty.

You think they were desperate enough to take any kind of measure to get help?

Oh, yes; they took an interest. You can tell whenever they were stopping trucks, they had the people out there. They were effective. There's no question about that. When better times returned, the Farm Holiday, I suppose, had served its purpose, so the interest dwindled. Then the Farmers Union became the strong farm organization.

Did people around this community look at the Holiday people as lawbreakers for stopping traffic?

No, I don't think so.

They had a lot of community support?

Yes, I know I read where there really was a fascist movement in some of the national magazines here that you probably have read too.

But you didn't think they were fascists?

No, I knew they weren't. They probably have some other tactics. I wouldn't question that.

Were you ever called a communist or fascist when you were out selling?

No.

Was the community of Lake Lillian pretty well sympathetic to the Holiday?

Yes.

How about Willmar?

I think they weren't too bad. This was like being the National Farm Organization now. Of course, I think the city of Willmar is more sympathetic to them than they were at that time to the Farm Holiday. At that time they didn't help the Farm Holiday, like advertising or donating money, like they do to the NFO at the present time. I don't know why they do that, unless they see no danger in NFO.

Maybe they see that as a less radical group?

Yes, it's supposed to be a radical group. They probably aren't so radical. I'm not a member of the NFO, but I sympathize with them.

What was the relationship between the Farm Holiday and the Farmers Union at this period.

I think they worked close together.

Most of the same people belonged to both.

I think the Bosches were Farmers Union. Hemming Nelson was Farmers Union.

What in your view did it accomplish?

Well, for one thing it prevented foreclosures on the farms. You would have seen numerous more farm foreclosures. It was very easy for the creditors or those who had the mortgages to start the foreclosure. The farmers had no chance to get a loan, from, say, another bank. This prevented wholesale foreclosure. I'm positive that it did a lot of good. . . .

But in the thirties did the government ever start producing some support [for cost of production] at least?

During the thirties, yes.

Do you think part of that was due to the Holiday?

Well, Roosevelt was the president. He was sympathetic. I think the country was in such bad shape at that time. The farmers did have congressmen who were quite able to speak for them.

How do you think Olson was as a governor? Was he an effective governor?

Very effective.

Was he a friend to the farmer?

Yes. Oh, yes, I think a real friend. Of course, he was also a politician, which is necessary. If he could be way ahead of the public with his ideas, then he would have to back up if it were a little bit too radical. Like the campaign in '34, was it? Where they wrote such a radical platform? It wasn't radical, but they had too many things in there. Of course, you can always interpret it differently. Take the . . . . well, we like to call them the radical element, they like to have everything black and white. Politically, it's not wise to have everything down. After you win an election you can always get those things. It probably isn't the most honest thing to do.

Reese, John
S433

Mr. Reese was born and raised on the farm where presently lives. His parents were Norwegian and Swedish immigrants. John is a farmer.

Do you have any recollection of Governor Floyd Olson?

Oh, yes.

How do you evaluate him?

I think Floyd Olson was a very good man. I remember one time that we had a meeting here at the — it was at the nearest grove, that's where we had the meeting, just east of here about seven miles — and Floyd Olson, he came there and there were a lot of people there thinking strongly of getting Tom Davis as a candidate for Governor. And I think there was a little bit of hostile feeling when he first came there, but nobody knew him. But as he got up and spoke, you could see the way he changed the crowd. They started applauding more and more all the time 'til they had just about everybody — well in fact he had everybody there on his side, 'cause he was a good speaker and he had good material, and it fitted into the condition.

You considered him a friend of the farmer?

Yes, he was, and also labor.

Labor, too. Was there much of a coalition between the farmers and the labor movement; I mean was it difficult to get those two groups together, did they seem to have a common interest?

Not a great deal. I think that it was played up by big business. That's the thing it was, it was played up by big business trying to divide them. They tell them that you can't be with labor, because labor ain't going to work for you and help you, and then they tell labor that you got to look out for the farmer as he gets too strong. And it's been one of the drawbacks for advancement of agriculture, that they had thrown stumbling blocks in the way of the farmer to get justice. The farmer has never really had justice. I'll say this, that if you can think of anything in the whole world worse than the position the farmer's in. He goes to town with his produce and he asks them how much are they going to give for it; then he goes to buy some things and he asks them how much they would have for it. It's no wonder he gets hump-backed. There's nothing in the world that's more unfair than that. You can't name it. That's the position that the farmer has been in all the time. And they spend millions of dollars every year to divide the farmers. If they'd once get together, there'd be a fair deal for all of agriculture.

Do you recall the depression of 1929?

Oh, yes. We had just bought the farm then at a good price and my dad, he got...I took a loan and paid him off, and there the slump came. But I put up quite a struggle. I made up my mind I was not going to lose out and my first move was going into turkeys. I knew the rich people would at least eat turkeys in the country, so I started raising turkeys and we made some money with them, too.

Even during the depression?

Yes, the banker . . . I was doing the banking in St. Leo then. Some people would be surprised on this, but we actually at one time had two banks in St. Leo, with a population of only about 60 people! But one quit and then the other one was standing there. I did my own banking there. And he says to me one day, he says, "You the only one in the country that's making any money." Because I was making money with these turkeys. And I was quite successful with them. I sold eggs to a hatchery and I guaranteed them 90% fertility, and he said, "If you can guarantee 90% fertility, we'll give you," I think it was, "17 or 18 cents apiece for the eggs." And after the season was over, he called me up and told me to come down there, he wanted to see me and talk to me. So I went down there to Worthington, where they took the eggs. We delivered to Marshall and then they would come there and get them and take them to Worthington. So, I went down there and he took me around there and introduced me to all of his men working there. "Here's the guy," he says, "that furnished us them 90% fertility eggs." That was pretty well done, you know; of course, I had to study how to do it, you had to . . . I'm not going to mention just the method I used, but anyway the ones I did were successful, which was the main thing, anyway.

During that time, were your neighbors making out as well?

No, they weren't.

What was the kind of sentiment of the people in the countryside; how were they reacting to the hard times?

Well, they were helpless; there wasn't much they could do.

Did you know any of the neighbors who lost any farms?

Oh, yes, there's quite a lot of them that lost their farms. But partly their own fault that they lost these farms, because if they'd have hung onto them and not given up, they could have got into that moratorium. We would have never had a moratorium probably in the United States if it hadn't been for the legislator, I mean, for the legislators group in North Dakota. They went to Washington and laid this plan out there that they should have a moratorium: anybody that had not lost his farm for more time than two years, he could redeem it. There was many of them that redeemed it. They could all have done it, perhaps, if they'd have stuck, but a lot of them got panicky and give up and just threw up the hands and they let them have it.

Was there much support in Minnesota for that moratorium? Was there much political agitation here for that idea, do you remember?

Yah, it was enacted so quickly that there wasn't any; it was almost a surprise to the people.

Well, John, the Holiday Association had quite a bit to do with that moratorium coming because after that deal in Marshall, Washington saw there was real unrest out in the Midwest and they got scared, and Franklin Roosevelt introduced the farm moratorium right away. They had been working for it, but they hadn't gotten it.

That's right. But the idea came from North Dakota.

Do you remember the Farmers' Holiday Association? Were you at all active in that, or . . . ?

Oh, I was quite active. It was good organization; I remember the instances where they had these sales and they stopped the sales.

Did you ever attend any sessions where they stopped any sales?

Oh, yes. I went to Granite Falls where they were foreclosing on a farm and the method they used — they just crowded. The sheriff was to sell it, because he was the auctioneer for it, and they would crowd him into a corner, never say a word, they just crowded him until he was right over in the corner, and then he could see that he couldn't do anything, so he called off the sale. I remember one instance — it was in Clarkfield — that I'd like to mention. It was the Farm Holiday had a meeting there and one of the county commissioners had come up with the idea that they should not let them stop these sales, that they should even call in the National Guard, if necessary, to enforce the sale. The reason I'd like to mention this is to show what humanity can do if they got the right heart. When this came up, this same county commissioner, he didn't think he was going to lose his farm, but they were foreclosing on the farm and he never asked for help. He was too proud to do that, because he wanted the sales to go on. So they voted by ballot at that meeting whether they should help him save his farm or should let him go by the wayside. And every vote there was to help him. And I thought that was one of the nicest things I've seen in my lifetime of people in a group, that they were all willing to help him, and he had been against them.

How did he respond when he got their help?

Oh, he was very well happy about that, of course.

Was he still . . . ?

They didn't even foreclose on him because they didn't care.

Did he go through a change of heart, too, then?

I don't know whether . . . oh, I don't think it didn't affect him that way, but he wasn't too bad a guy in the first place anyhow. The only thing, I guess, he wanted the laws enforced, and of course this was illegal, what they did there, you know. But it sometimes looks as though you have to do something illegal to get something done that is right.

Do you think there were many farmers that were ready for, you know, really kind of revolutionary activity at that period of time, in the twenties, late twenties, early thirties? I mean, would they have defied the National Guard if the National Guard come out to help?

No, they would not. They had respect for the government that way. Yeh, but they had stopped sales where they had trouble. It had been up here northwest here — one town, I don't remember the name of the town, but it was along side of a small town — that they foreclosed on a farmer, and the livestock was to be sold. They used this penny sale: they would bid their penny or a dime on an animal and then nobody else would bid, that would be the only bid. In one instance it happened up there that I knew the party, but I can't remember the name just now. But anyway, he was there and he made his low bid and the sheriff, the deputy sheriff, went over there and was going to take him out of the crowd, you see, because he figured that was disrupting the sale by bidding such a low bid. And so he resisted, and the sheriff shot him in the face with this blinding stuff — whatever it was, I don't know. But anyway, it knocked him out, see, and he fell down. And right away they grabbed that sheriff, disarmed him, and they went on after that and had the sale. And the sale didn't bring but just very little because they made them put the sale through. It was advertised, and they made them put it through, and they put it through, and then when they was through, they gave all the property back the next day. They gave it back to the guy that had the sale.

How did the bankers feel about sales like that?

Well, that cured some of the bankers! It did. I imagine, though, that there were some bankers that had sympathy with the people, but under them circumstances why, you know, they no doubt like to see it go through — the sales, I mean.

Were most of the farms in this area mortgaged to insurance companies at that time? Did the insurance companies hold most of the mortgages?

The county treasurer told me at that time 70% of the farmers in our county were subject to foreclosure, one way or

JOHN REESE

the other, not having paid their taxes or delinquent on the mortgage.

Was the condition about the same on the machinery, too?

No, it wasn't so much on the machinery as it was on the land, but they did have mortgage on machinery, too, of course. Some of them, not all of them.

Do you think the Farm Holiday movement made any accomplishments or brought about any accomplishments for American agriculture?

Yes, I do. In this way, that it brought attention to conditions that farmers were in and it went quite a ways, because it was unfair. They had no control over the prices; prices went down to practically nothing. I myself sold hogs for seven dollars apiece and that was the government buying them. Otherwise they would only have brought about two dollars apiece. But the government was out buying up this, what they called, the pigs, see, and had them shipped in. What they did with them, whether they destroyed them or butchered them, I don't know. But anyway, in order to give the farmer a little something to buy groceries with anyway.

Now, this would have been after Roosevelt came in, to ship away when they were buying them up?

Yes. I remember one party that had fat cattle and they shipped them and they only got about eight dollars apiece, for fat cattle. The guy shipped the cows with the sheep, and when he got the returns, I mean they sent him the returns of the sheep and they said he owed some money, that it didn't cover the expenses! So then he said, I haven't got no money, but I got more sheep.

John, what did you hear about the Farm Holiday when they went to Marshall? You were so involved, I'd say I was kind of surprised that you weren't down in Marshall. But what did you hear about Marshall; what in your mind took place in Marshall during those days?

Well, I met them about a mile north of town and then they had been down there one day first. Then there was too much opposition, see, for the few that was there, so the next day, they went back there and then they met some on a farm north of town. And they all marched in. I don't know how many there was, cause there was an awful lot of people, probably a thousand anyway — five thousand do you think? Maybe it was five thousand. And they marched into town and, of course, they were set up to give them a reception, the town was, they watered. . . .

Hoses?

Watered whatever you call that part. . . .

Fire Department?

And they was going to spray them with water, that's what I heard anyway, but they disconnected the hoses and they set the sheriff on his head and disarmed him. I knew the one guy that took the revolver away from him. But, then they marched down town. They would go in a restaurant and get lunch and they didn't even ask them to pay for the lunch, told them the lunch was on us, see? So they got treated better than they expected to be treated! So it wasn't all hostility at Marshall, either. Of course, over this, they wanted to close that big Swift plant and that's what started it, the agitation. But they did close up, too, for a while. But they didn't use that practice very much because it actually didn't accomplish much. And then the Governor stepped in that too at that time, and relief was in sight. A lot of people thought they'd wait and see if they did actually get help. They did get help — got that moratorium off and they eased up on foreclosing and they wouldn't have hardly any of that. But the Holiday movement, they had one unfortunate thing happen here at Canby — there was picketing, see, they were picketing and they used quite a few means of stopping anybody from coming in and marketing his produce. The thing about it was this, that a young man got killed there; he got shot.

How did that happen?

Well, I don't exactly like to give the true details on it because it involves some people. It was this way, that this farmer that shot this boy, I don't think he even knew he shot the boy. They had him in such condition, he went into town . . . I was told that they borrowed him a gun and told him to go out there and the first one that interfered, shoot him. And he went out there and this boy, he come over towards him and he shot him and killed him. That's how I had it related to me, anyhow. He was not happy over it afterwards, either, this farmer. They had a lawsuit, and he was acquitted . . . not a lawsuit, but he was charged and he was acquitted and afterwards. There was somebody drove by his home and they fired shots into his home and he was actually so scared and worried so much, I think it was the cause of his death.

Was that the only violence that you know of that was connected with that movement? On that kind of a scale?

Yes, it's the only one in this section, anyway.

A man at Montevideo lost one eye, you know.

Yah, but I'm not sure whether that was true or not. In fact, I don't think it was that way they said that he lost an eye. I don't think that he did loose no eye, because I knew the man and talked to him afterwards and he had both of his eyes. But you know, stories will get out!

When did the depression end for the farmers?

I'd like to say something more about this Holiday Association, then.

Sure.

You see, then, after these things got pretty well in the hands of the government and things were going quite well, they had a meeting in Clarkfield discussing whether they should dissolve the organization. And I made a motion that we should dissolve the organization. I says, "We only lost one life; we could have lost many more," I says, "if we kept on." And I says, "We really have accomplished what we intended to do and let's dissolve it." And they did dissolve it; it was just dissolved entirely in the whole state.

This would have been, what, about late thirties?

Oh, you know the date probably.

Marshall was in '34.

Now this was the year afterwards, '35, then.

'35 Or so?

Yup.

When do you think the depression ended for the farmer?

It has never ended!

It's never ended!

No.

O.K.

The farmer's still having problems and he's still under that hammer yet, and he will be until he gets organized so that he can help himself. Because if nobody's going to help him, he's got to help himself. One thing bad about politics is this: that they look up to a higher authority, like their leader, and if they do that long enough, the rank and file loose interest. I want to cite something that happened right here now. I attend most of their meetings, and the last two meetings that we had in Clarkfield called for the hall, there wasn't enough people here, so we met in a car. We didn't use the hall at all, just met in a car! Something has got to happen to get these people to see what they have to do or to get them active again. I think this Watergate was the greatest thing that happened since the Revolutionary War. I made that remark right away when it happened. And very little credit is given to the deputy, the young colored man that discovered this tape on the doors. If it hadn't been for him discovering that, he called in the police, they might have got by with it for an awful long time and never even been caught.

John Bosch, photo by Dan Setterberg, August 21, 1972.

Bosch, John
S178

John Bosch was instrumental to the organization of the Minnesota Farm Holiday Association. He served as president of the state organization. Mr. Bosch lived in the Willmar area and was an insurance man for many years. He passed away in 1978 at the age of 79.

Will you tell us a little bit about the origins and motivations of the Holiday Organization, Mr. Bosch?

Well, if this is agreeable, I'll try to start as the thing started with my relationship to the Farm Holiday Association. It doesn't make any difference how hard you work — if you incur a debt, when say corn is 80 cents a bushel and you try to pay for it when it is 2 cents a bushel, it doesn't make any difference how hard you work, you can't do it. Well, this was the situation that existed through almost all of the most productive agricultural area in the United States [in the 1930's]. Some thirteen states in the upper part of the United States produce approximately 90 percent of the total food supply. And farmers were losing their farms — in some counties as high as 90 percent of the farmers had already lost their farms.

And you're probably familiar with what they call the quantity theory of money — the value of money and credit relative to the business to be transacted determines the relationship. If you've got $100 to measure the value of 100 bushels of wheat, it's a dollar to the bushel. If you've got $10, it's 10 bushels to the dollar and so on. Well, if people get into debt on the basis of an inflated currency and inflated credit and then are compelled to pay when these have been withdrawn, they can't pay. And as I was saying something like 90 percent of the farmers had already lost their farms. Well, my father was a very good friend of Hemming Nelson, who was vice president of the Farmers Union of the state of Minnesota. And at my father's request I joined the Farmers Union. I became active in the Lake Elizabeth Township unit and later became the county president of the Farmers Union.

When did your first association with that begin? What year?

Well, that would have been about 1930.

This would have been in the Willmar Area?

Yes, the Willmar area. And meeting with these people and discussing things about it and having some concept of history and economics and so forth — my father was well informed in this field — I put together for Kandiyohi County an idea. After all, food — you can't do without food. You can do without cars, you can do without lots of things, but you can't do without food. And the ability to control the flow of whatever you have to sell to the market, within general economic conditions, will determine the price. This is axiomatic in economics. So I put together an idea: four things that we would do. And if we did not get them we would then strike, we would then refuse to sell anything.

One of them was immediate: we had the bank holiday. One was an immediate holiday of foreclosures. Another was cost of production for farm products. One of them was the abolition of the Federal Reserve System, which was in the main responsible for these fluctuations in monies and credits and the tremendous variation in prices. And the fourth one was that in the event of another war, all profits deriving from war production would be taxed 100 percent. Now these were the four things; I presented this to the Lake Elizabeth Township meeting. It covers a broad area. Nevertheless these were four — if you looked for four, you probably couldn't find more important things as far as economics, the general economic health is concerned. But I presented this to the Lake Elizabeth meeting and they voted that I be permitted to present it to the county meeting, Kandiyohi County. Which I did. Kandiyohi voted to send me to the next state convention of the Minnesota Farmers Union and present it there. I did and I had developed a pretty good talk in connection with it.

Do you recall what year this would be?

I think this would have been in '31. It was either '31 or '32. And I presented it to the state convention, and I'll tell you it took the house down. Really! They voted 100 percent that I be sent, taken to the national convention and that I present this same program to the national convention, which was held in Oklahoma City. So I got to be the chairman of the resolutions committee at that convention . . . no, the secretary, pardon me, the secretary of the resolutions committee at that convention. And one of the things I then presented was a resolution in connection with this. I would make the speech, I would present the thing, and these would be our four demands, or if this was not done within a reasonable length of time, we then would call a farm strike.

Well, while as far as they were concerned they were for it, they were at the same time afraid. The Farmers Union had become, and this is good, quite heavily involved in co-operatives, business of various kinds. And they were afraid if they became involved in this that legally these co-operatives might be involved in it also. So instead of getting the endorsement of the national Farmers Union at their convention, they did pass a resolution to call a convention for the expressed purpose of building an organization.

Well, this convention was called in Des Moines, and there were representatives from pretty well all over the country. And Milo Reno was elected president of the national Farm Holiday Association. This name was selected because we did have the bank holiday, and we wanted a farm holiday. And the program I had set up became the program. Well, Milo Reno was quite well known, because he had been president of the Farmers Union in Iowa for quite awhile and I was relatively new. And as far as I was concerned, this suited me better, because I did less traveling than he did, and I had these little children, which was quite a responsibility on my part. Well, what would have happened if everything had gone according to schedule, I don't know. But what did happen was that different areas, knowing that this meeting was being held and that we were probably going to call a farm strike . . . there were half a dozen areas that called strikes of their own. Just blocked the highway and not related to anything . . . somebody . . . maybe he wanted the publicity or whatever his reason was, or maybe his reasons were entirely honorable and good, but anyhow there were a half a dozen or more of these. Omaha, there was one around Omaha. There was one around Sioux City and different places all over.

Was there one at Worthington at this stage?

That was different. It wasn't in the nature of . . . Marshall had one where they had quite a rumpus. As far as Worthington was concerned, if there was one, it was not of enough consequence that I recall it. But here something develops which would be difficult to foresee. A farmer, by the nature of his occupation, is an individual. His farm is different than somebody else's farm — the nature of the soil, the amount of rain he gets or doesn't get, the size of his family, the sex of his family, the age of his family, his inclination, does he feed cattle or does he raise grain, and the date he has to pay doesn't fit with everybody else's date. Well, to try to fit these all together is an extremely difficult thing. And not only is that difficult, you began to set up terrific conflicts between the different groups. So what should have been your support becomes you opposition. We tried it, then we called it off because it was spasmodic, intermittent. We called it off and set another date where we were all supposed to do it together. And on that date, I don't recall that date, but on that date everybody was supposed to do it together. Now here in Minnesota we were doing a pretty good job. There was doggone little flowing to South St. Paul or anywhere else.

Who was helping you here in Minnesota? You were the main driver?

Well, as far as the program was concerned and the things that were accomplished, at least 50 percent of the paid-up membership of the national Farm Holiday Association came from Minnesota. All the rest of the United States had less than half. So we were supporting what everybody else was or wasn't trying to do. And this became a factor a little bit later, too. Well, we were making progress. We met Governor Floyd Olson who was 100 percent in favor of what we were trying to do. We were very, very close personal friends. In fact, when he died, I was one of five people who he asked to see him on his deathbed. I didn't get the message until it was too late, but we were about as close as people can be. So Floyd Olson did everything and anything he could, as did Bill Langer of North Dakota. But none of the rest of the governors had the guts to . . . Schmedeman of Wisconsin, Berry of South Dakota, Herring of Iowa, yes, none of these ever did anything.

Nebraska?

Nebraska never did anything about it. So it became apparent that much as we wanted to, we were not having much impact on the market because of these various things. And it's so different. We followed organized labor, which we had to do. We were the only farm organization that ever fed labor while it was on strike. And this terrific strike which they had here in Minneapolis, Local 544 was about to get started.

Was this the Teamsters' Strike?

Yes. Well, people were killed in connection with it. And I was one of the speakers at their memorial funeral. But, say Honeywell, 5,000 people working in the same place. They sell their time. Honeywell buys it. It costs them 25 cents to get on the streetcar as it was then, or the bus now, to go to a place of meeting. Well, the farmer maybe it's the middle of harvest, or maybe there's a snowstorm. If you get the farmers together on the basis of their diversity of interests from the standpoint of controlling the flow, it didn't take long, as far as I was concerned, to see that we were getting nowhere with it, much as we ought to have, theoretically should have, but just couldn't.

Well, there was a Farmers Union meeting in Lake Elizabeth Township and a man came to this meeting. And believe it or not, his name was Robert E. Lee. He was a widower and he had moved from one county to another. And he had a chattel mortgage. He didn't know that a chattel mortgage provided that if he did move from one county to another without the consent of the mortgage holder, they could foreclose. And this is what they were doing. Well, I said to the people there that this just isn't fair. And in this township, we won't let it happen. So I said, I'll get up really early and I will drive to where this man [the mortgage holder] lives—he was a banker—and try to talk him out of it. But just in case I can't, go up and down and cross over, go another six miles, cover four townships and ask every farmer to be there. And if they insist on selling it we'll buy it for pennies and give it back.

Well, I got to him, all right, but I couldn't move him. So here comes the sheriff, Paul Anderson, six feet four, a big, powerful fellow, and the fellow that held the mortgage. Here was the whole community, everyone standing there with pitchforks. They had nooses hanging through the branches of the trees. They took one look and began to leave.

Which county?

This was in Kandiyohi County. In Lake Elizabeth Township. So he stopped at a bank in Willmar and he sold the mortgage to them. So we stopped this. Well, I had talked all this over with Governor Floyd Olson and I had an arrangement with him that as far as the sheriff was concerned, that if the sheriff would call him, say there was a probability of trouble, then he would relieve the sheriff, which would then protect his bond holders. Well, it wasn't too long after that again in Lake

Elizabeth Township a fellow by the name of Ben Thomas, a farmer, and this was a real estate mortgage and they were foreclosing. And I suppose I had a thousand farmers in Willmar on that day and I told Paul Anderson, the sheriff, what Floyd Olson had said, if he called him, he would be relieved of responsibility.

He said, "Well, it doesn't make any difference how I sympathize, I've sworn to uphold the law and I've got to do it."

Well, I had made arrangements with eight powerful men, one was a brother of mine . . . .

Would this have been Richard?

No, Herbert. He's quite a bit heavier and stronger. Fritz Krangenbring was another; he's dead now, as are nearly all of the people who helped to do this. Two men for each arm and two men for each leg. And when the hour came to try the sale and I couldn't convince him to call the governor, he said, "Well, gentlemen" and the next second he was flat on his back on the floor. And he stayed there. We decided that he would stay there until we said he would have to leave town. He asked if he could join, so we did give him an honorary membership.

This was the sheriff?

This was the sheriff. Well, this we did pretty well all over. Now, the only other place they did succeed in doing it was to some extent in North Dakota and in Minnesota. But the entire impact of the stopping foreclosures was in Minnesota. In fact, our family still has 80 acres of timber along Lake Elizabeth, in Lake Elizabeth Township. Where they tried this in Iowa, they had to flee the state. And we had a little cabin where we had a man who had worked in our family for quite a long time, until he got to be fairly old and we had retired him in that cabin that we built for him in the woods. We had about half a dozen people from Iowa who fled the state because they had tried to stop a sale and couldn't make it. And they stayed there until we worked out something.

If I could just interrupt you here for a question on your technique: Did you actually stop these sales, or did you carry them on then with the penny auction kind of tactics?

We did both. If we felt there was good publicity in having a penny sale . . . well, I'll tell you. the news got out, and a lot of people that were thinking of foreclosures thought, "Well, this is no good." Or on the other hand, if we felt that we, from the standpoint of good publicity, just to say "Well, there's going to be no more. We've got the bank holiday and son of a gun, there's going to be a foreclosure holiday." An so we pretty well had it stopped all through the state of Minnesota, although the farther you went south, this is relatively a richer area and there was less there. We were less powerful there.

There was more activity around Kandiyohi County.

Kandiyohi County, Chippewa County, Yellow Medicine County, actually Lac Qui Parle, those counties.

And you were in pretty good contact with Harry Haugland?

Oh, somewhere along here I was going to mention the names. But the backbone of the thing—Harry Haugland, Merle Porter . . . C.A. Winslow, and George Windingstad, the Smalgaards, and, oh, there were probably about a dozen. Just terrific, terrific fellows.

Just something in between here . . . in 1969, the University of Minnesota received a federal grant. The purpose of this was to make a backwards study, a historical study from the time the first white man came to the upper part of the United States up to the current date. And they put together a three-hour movie, and the title of it is *The Roots Of Reform.* E.W.

Ziebarth is the narrator, and I have more time in that movie than any other person. And when E.W. Ziebarth summarizes, in the last ten minutes or so of the three hours, he names about a dozen people who, in the opinion of their research for the background, had contributed the most to create the climate of progress, and I'm one of them.

Well, I thought this was important enough so I took off a week and drove through this whole doggone area to try to find the people who were the background, the backbone of this thing and made it possible. Well, Merle Porter was dead, Harry Haugland was alive — he had had a stroke and it was rather difficult to carry on a conversation with him. Carl Barkus probably was the best of all — I mean, just from the standpoint of an absolutely immovable solid — and he and his wife lived in a rest home. I hadn't seen them for probably fifteen years. And he and his wife were sitting there in their room in this rest home. And when I came in, I just stood in the doorway and didn't say anything. And he just looked and looked and looked, and finally he hollered, "John! John!" And he got up and threw his arms around me and just cried and cried.

Well, anyway I did the best I could to share it with him, the opinion of others. What we had done then was considered very important. And somewhere there is suppose to be — I've never seen it, but Floyd Olson told me about it — a letter from the President, President Roosevelt, to Floyd Olson asking him to tell me that in his opinion, we had done more to create the climate of progress than anybody else in the United States.

Well, anyway, we stopped this foreclosure in Kandiyohi County and through Chippewa County and pretty well all over. In fact, in many instances all we needed to do was say, "I'll call John Bosch. He's on his way." That would do it.

And this finally — there are three ways to foreclose: one is through your local sheriff. Well, we had no problem. There were exactly the same tactics where I had eight men, this was down in Ivanhoe, there was a foreclosure. Little bit of a fellow; he was so scared, he couldn't even stand. So we had to hold him. And he was being foreclosed and again a big powerful guy was the sheriff, and again I tried to talk to him, but didn't succeed. I remember George Windingstad and Carl Barkus were both there, and there was a little excitement, and he was down on his back. Well, after it was over he was grateful really that we had stopped him from doing it. He knew it shouldn't have been done, that it was wrong. So he asked to join, so we gave him a membership. And then finally this got to the point where we had the state of Minnesota, we had a march on the capitol.

Let me just start you off here with a little question: I'm very interested in the tactics of disarming sheriffs and disrupting sales and so forth. You couldn't really have done this without the cooperation of the governor, could you?

Well, none of the other states, except North Dakota, succeeded because the governor did nothing in the way of cooperation.

The governor could have sent troops or something to stop you.

I talked this over with him at great length. I said, "If we do it this way, there is going to be no great problem. But if you're going to send troops, you're going to have a civil war." And as I was about to say we had this tremendous march on the capitol. We were demanding a moratorium on foreclosures.

This would have been '32?

I suppose it would. Floyd Olson was governor.

March, '32.

JOHN BOSCH

Yeah and oh, man, we had a big one. From the old depot right down to the state capitol from curb to curb solid. And I'll show you some pictures. Up at the capitol there you see big bronze horses [pointing to picture].

'33. Was that the picture down here?

Yeah. That's part of the . . .

That's Nebraska, I think, but this was the St. Paul march that you're talking about. It's back as far as one can see.

Well, this doesn't . . .

That's not a very good picture.

No. Well, see they had some different place, central Minnesota. Up on the capitol, up on the front there there are three huge bronze horses and somewhere I have a picture of Governor Floyd B. Olson and myself standing up there. And anyway, the principal thing we asked for was a mortgage moratorium, which we got. And North Dakota did the same thing. And Bill Langer, who later became senator, well, he was a flamboyant type of person. Nevertheless, I had a whale of a lot of respect for him. Senator Frazier was anything but a public speaker, but just from the standpoint of his honesty and nature they'd be pretty damn sure he was on the right side. He was hard to beat. Well, Bill Lemke was a little more volatile and he became the candidate for Father Coughlin, you know. But they had some tremendously good people there in North Dakota. So now we had two states where we had mortgage moratoriums.

Well, there are three ways to foreclose. One is through your local sheriff, and one is through your district judge, and one is through the federal courts. There was this one company where we stopped them with the sheriff and we'd stopped them in district court. As far as the sheriff was concerned, if he tried anything, the next second he was taking a nap on the floor. I don't mean literally taking a nap, but he was on the floor. But with a judge we generally escorted him to the can and closed the door.

You actually did this?

Oh, yes, oh yes. And well . . . so this particular day in Montevideo they were foreclosing in federal court. A U.S. marshall was there, and I bet I had about 10,000 farmers there. Well, I never tried to conceal who I was, and I had never met this fellow before so I came in and introduced myself. And we had developed tactics, techniques and so on. I told him that I felt that if he would let me talk to him, that I could convince him that he should not proceed with the sale.

"Well," he said, "it doesn't make any difference how much I agree with you, I must proceed with the sale."

Well, out in the hall where you couldn't identify somebody, somebody would holler, "Let the son of a bitch out here and we'll cut a hole in the ice and push him down twice and pull him up once." Somebody else would say, "Let's tie him up with one hind leg behind the car and haul him back to St. Paul," and this type of thing and he was white as a sheet.

Well, it's a fact we never hurt anybody. Well, finally he called the U.S. district attorney and I asked him if I could talk, and I said, "Now you can be awfully brave, but there's going to be no sale. If you call it off, fine, but if you want us to manhandle him, if we have to, we have to. But there's going to be no sale." So they called it off.

Well, not long after that I got a call from Floyd Olson. "John, I'd like to see you." So I came in and he said, "John, I had a call from the President, he told me to tell you specifically that he knows you and I know him. He thinks you're doing a tremendous job, but you can't buck the federal government."

Well, I said, "Floyd, we did."

And he said, "You're going to spend the rest of your life in the pen."

And I said, "Now, Floyd, up to now we've hurt no one. You can put me in the pen, but if it takes 10,000, if it takes 100,000, if it takes I don't know how many, I'm not going to stay there. If you want a civil war, if that's what you're aiming for, that's the way to get it."

"Well," he said, "What do you want me to do?"

I said, "Well, call the President." Which he did. So here was the President in Washington, Floyd Olson was on one phone, and I was on the other. And the President told me, "Mr. Bosch, I can't tell you how much I admire what you're doing" — I don't remember his exact words but something like that — "but you can't buck the United States government."

But again I said, "Mr. President, we did."

And he said, "I don't want you to spend the rest of your life in the penitentiary."

I told him the same thing I told Floyd Olson: "Up to now no one has been hurt, but we are stopping them. We are not going to let the farmer be the butt of what was planned."

So then he said, "What do you want me to do?"

And I said, "There are three things we offer anyone who wants to foreclose: one, we'll give you the deed but you give back a mortgage to the farmer for the amount he's got in it, and you farm for awhile and see how you like it; two, you . . . accept the number of dollars that are equal to the amount that would be purchased by the number of bushels — at the time they borrowed. If you borrow money when corn is 80 cents a bushel an you try to pay for it when it is 2 cents a bushel, it doesn't make any difference how you try, you can't . . . ."

So scale the debt down accordingly?

Right! Or leave it all in the Federal Land Bank, and see if the Federal Land Bank offered them some kind of a compromise, or otherwise tell them to go to hell. That's what we did. So they let you know. And we called Henry Wallace and Henry Wallace said the Federal Land Bank called him and called the thing off. Now that's the last time they tried.

In district court?

In district court. And not long after that we got through Congress the Federal Debt Conciliation Commission Act.

So you think your actions in Minnesota precipitated that act?

I know it! I know it.

Mr. Bosch, could I ask you another question here? When you talked to Governor Olson and the President, and they were a little bit upset about your tactics at Montevideo, did you get any indication from either the Governor, particularly Governor Olson, how much pressure he had from financial institutions, or insurance companies to push against you people? I mean, how much pressure was there on the other side?

I think he had a very considerable. And on different occasions he talked about it and there were a number of things that came up periodically, not only this. In fact after it got to the point where he really had a lot of pressure, why Floyd would give me a call to come in and we'd plan something. But what I asked him to do in connection with any of this was, don't argue with them. Tell them to go talk to me. I'm the criminal in the thing, if that's what you want to call it. You aren't, I am. Let them talk. As a part of this, a representative — maybe I made a mistake on this — a representative of the American Manufacturer's Association came down from New York. He was the vice president. And he said, "Mr. Bosch, I will give

JOHN BOSCH

you $1,000,000 if you will use this organization you've built to fight organized labor." I should have taken it [laughter]. No, that's right, I should have.

You really think so?

Yes. I should have given $100,000 to the labor union and I should have said, "I will keep you quietly informed; you give me insurance contracts in connection with this." And I'd have $900,000 to finance what I'm doing. Well, another thing, a group of investors — and I don't know any of their names — but a man came out to visit me on the farm, and then he said, "Mr. Bosch, I represent some very wealthy people in the Twin Cities area. Now if you will let them pick out the farms to foreclose on — 100; 1000; 10,000 throughout the United States — they can pick these up for nothing. All they need to do is add their name to it, they've got the financial backing. We'll make you a full owner." Yeah, I should have done that, too. But I didn't do [that] either.

Well, that Conciliation Commissioner's Act, in and of itself — what it did, it provided that any debtor and/or creditor could appeal to the commissioners, who were recommended by the governors and appointed by the President. And in this area I picked them, the governors approved them and they were sent on to the President. But you could appeal to the Debt Conciliation Commissioner and he could listen to the story and he could set aside the terms of the mortgage on whatever basis he felt would be reasonably equitable. And if a person would say, "Well, I can't pay a thousand dollars, but I can pay ninety . . . these are the reasons why, and that is all I can pay." Bang [hits table] that's what it was.

Well, it is not an exaggeration to say that through what we did — the National Farm Holiday Association bringing about the mortgage moratorium in North Dakota and Minnesota and the Debt Conciliation Commission Act — I don't think it's an exaggeration to say that we probably saved hundreds of thousands or millions of homes and farms from foreclosure. I don't think that's an exaggeration.

Then you see really the foreclosure movement as being far more productive of real good than all the publicity that Reno was attracting in Iowa?

Well, what were the things that were accomplished by this? Well, as far as I am concerned I don't know of any. They never had a mortgage moratorium going, they never stopped any foreclosure sales, they were less successful in most other areas such as stopping the flow of commodities to the market. But he did have a substantial public appeal. He was a dynamic speaker. He had a place in it.

Would you go so far as to say he was a demagogue?

Oh, no. I don't think he knew much of anything about history; I don't think he knew much about economics. I think he felt the public pulse and his sympathy, as far as I'm concerned, I think his sympathy was in the right direction. At the same time, I don't think he knew too much — well, like I say, the time he wanted to call a conference of Huey Long, Father Coughlin, and himself, and Governor Olson to take over the United States! Take these components and try to put together to run a country — I mean, what could be a more fantastic thing than that? When he began to become involved in this type of thing, I told him that I was not going to continue to support the national organization. So we stopped sending in any membership fees, that portion of the membership fee that went to the national.

11½ cents?

Yeah. We stopped sending any money to the national.

When would that have been? '34 or '35?

This would have been . . .

Closer to '36, wouldn't it? You chaired the '36 convention?

Well yes, I did.

That was after Reno's death, so it must have been '34 or '35.

Yes, it must have been in there. And we had quite a conference on that, and he laid down the law to me, and I laid down the law to him. I explained and said that as far as I was concerned to continue to pay from Minnesota money to the national organization which was doing things that as far as we were concerned we felt were not productive of anything that would be good for the country or for agriculture, we wouldn't allow. We just wouldn't. And we didn't. And he died, and of course since I was vice president, I automatically became president.

Well, because of the cost of travel when we set up the National Farm Holiday Association, the total vote of any state was invested in the president and every one was equal. So then when we had a convention, we had it at the state office building here in St. Paul, the actual convention of the Farm Holiday Association. Well, they had all kinds of presidents; each one had the same vote as we with all of the membership. Well, that's a different thing. Anyhow the question came up immediately as to whether or not they would control the convention because they had these votes, or whether or not at any convention the membership themselves controlled it. Who was to make the decision? Me! So when this question came up, I ruled that when an organization is in convention assembled, the members control that convention. They would have an equal opportunity with anybody else on any subjects they wanted. There were eleven presidents there, and on every issue of any consequence they had to vote each equal. I mean there were states that had never had a member except the president. So then they withdrew and had a separate convention.

How many would that have been?

As I recall eleven other states.

All eleven of them withdrew?

All eleven of them.

So this was virtually a Minnesota convention?

This left Minnesota. We had a lot of members from the other states.

In the Minnesota chapter?

No. They came.

They came to the convention?

Yes. They came to the convention and they stayed when the presidents left. Because they had a vote that they didn't have if they went with him.

So you would estimate that your convention wasn't really greatly weakened by that walk-out in 1936?

It wasn't weakened at all. It wasn't weakened at all.

Maybe strengthened?

In a way, probably.

It was the discipline and the membership.

Well, as far as I was concerned it was not a happy situation, but it isn't what you want to happen. But the question, the principal question as far as they were concerned, they were in convention assembled for no other purpose than to endorse

Lemke [William Lemke of North Dakota for President of the U.S.]; this was the only thing they had in mind. And I wasn't about to, if I could stop it, to let this happen. Oh, it didn't become violent, but anyhow they walked out and I — that was the end of that.

What was your link that year? There are some who suggest that there was quite a strong tie with the convention that year and communist front organizations. Would you like to comment on the whole business of front organizations? The Farmer's National Committee for Action and others?

This is something I was going to ask you to cut it off and talk about a bit — whether you wanted me to bring it in or whether you don't. Now as far as I am concerned, I want to put it in.

Well if you do, let's leave it on.

At the time the Farm Holiday Association was organized, there was also in this area an organization called the United Farmer's League. And Len Harris was the head man of it. I became very well acquainted with him. He and his wife had dinner at our home several times and we had dinner at their home several times, and as far as a person was concerned I liked him and his wife also. He was a son of the vice president of the Chase National Bank of New York. He wanted to become a minister — now this is what he told me — he wanted to become a minister, and his father didn't want him to. So he sent him for a trip around the world. In connection with this trip he landed in Russia and he spent quite a while there, several years, and became a very ardent communist. Now he was the head in the United States of the agricultural arm of the Communist Party.

Now here's a peculiar thing: when we were going to stop a foreclosure sale, we couldn't stop them all, but if we wanted a lot of publicity we would pick somebody who was . . . well, very well respected in the community who had farmed hard, who had tried hard — where the whole community would support him — and we sent out the word. Brother they were there. Well, as far as the United Farmer's League is concerned, they tried to stop foreclosures, but they never stopped one of them. They would go through the motions, but they never stopped any.

And we were head-on collision. They would have people — we would have meetings of the farmers — they would always have somebody there to heckle. And I got pretty well accustomed what to do, and I could handle it pretty well. Well, this went on, until Germany invaded Poland and Russia and all of a sudden they came and said, "Now look, we've got to call this quits."

And another thing that was incidental to this: you're familiar with Harry Bridges [leader of the Longshoremen's Union]. I was present at the meeting at the Nicollet Hotel during the beginning of the war where Harry Bridges moved that the function of every progressive in the United States was to keep the United States out of the war. Never, never let us get in. The week after Russia was invaded, here was Harry Bridges back at the same Nicollet Hotel. Now we had to get in it.

I've got a book over there that's called *The Progressive,* if you've heard of it. I knew Elmer Benson way, way back when he was still in the bank in Appleton. You know, one time I had spent the day working on a project at the state capitol. This was in the spring; it was still icy. On my way back, crossing Lake Street Bridge, the streetcar had to be stopped. And a man climbed up on the rail and he climbed down and he climbed up and he climbed down and he climbed up and he jumped. Well, I left my car on the bridge, and I ran to the end of the bridge, climbed down the bank and kicked off my shoes and coat and jumped in. I got to where he had gone down and I even got to about where I got a hold of him and I couldn't do it. If I had looked back, there was a federal patrol boat in the river. If I had seen it, I probably could have saved him. Anyway, I wasn't able to. I bet I had an audience of 2, 3, 5,000 people before I got back to the bank. And nobody climbed down the bank to even help me up. I was so all in, I couldn't climb out. The water was pretty sharp, because the Ford Dam was not too far below. And finally a car came with two people, and they pulled me out. The next morning I got a telephone call from Governor Benson: "John, was that really you that jumped in the river trying to save this guy from committing suicide?" I said yes.

"Well," he said, "I always thought you were a goddamned fool and now I know it."

Where did your idea of Ghandian nonviolent resistance come from?

From Ghandi himself. The philosophy which he had. As a total group, what were our weapons? The first weapon was food. You can get along without most anything except food. And if we would have been able to control the flow of food to the market, nothing would have been beyond what we demanded. You have to have it. But we were unable to do it. In order to control the flow of food to the market, farm produce to the market . . . if every farmer would have agreed to it, there would have been no activity, they'd just stay at home. But it didn't work that way, so there were quite a number of efforts at blocking the markets, and trying to stop it that way. Then there was the question of what extent would you run into law, what extent would you run into state militia. On this basis, we thought if it comes to this, as far as we're concerned, we will be subject to whatever violence they want to bring. We will not retaliate with it. As the British army found out, you can't keep doing that. Your stomach gets full of it, your conscience gets full and you quit. And as far as we were concerned, that if it did come to that, whatever they might project, if we didn't do anything back, they would have to quit that too.

So you were simply an early student of Ghandi? You were observing what Ghandi was doing in India?

We were prepared to use it if it evolved in that direction.

And what about the influence of your brother? John Schover [historian, author of Cornbelt Rebellion*] has called him the brightest economic thinker in the national Farm Holiday Association?*

I have no objection to him being called that. It's not accurate. From the standpoint of the Farm Holiday Association, what he did — I know this doesn't sound good — it derived from the organization. Richard is two years older than I am. He is a tremendous student. He always was. As far as I was concerned, I was always more active. I can't remember the time when we were kids when I couldn't run faster than he could. I was an active baseball player. I could husk corn 50 percent faster than he could. But as far as he was concerned, he was always a terrific student. He took correspondence courses.

At one point there was a very small college in Arkansas. The name of it was Commonwealth College. There were three of us at the same time farming together: Richard, myself and my brother Herbert. So he asked if we would undertake to run the farm. It was a pretty sizeable operation. He wanted to take a year off to find out if he wanted to go to school or not. He had gone one winter to an agricultural school; otherwise he had not gone to any other school. He never went to high school, but he was accepted as a student by Commonwealth College. And he went there one year, and John R. Commons was the president of Commonwealth College. He had studied economics. No, Commons was a professor of Economics at Madison, Wisconsin. A man by the name of William Zoic was president of Commonwealth College. Anyhow, he accepted Richard. At the end of the year he wrote some economic thesis. I don't know just what it was. Zoic was so impressed that he sent it on to Commons. Commons was so impressed that he accepted him as a student there. He went there one year, got a degree, and joined the faculty. At Wisconsin, yes. Then the depression came, and while he was one of the latest to join the faculty, there just wasn't enough money to keep him, so he was one of the first ones that was pared off from the payroll, and he came back farming and has been here ever since. From the standpoint of the economist, yes. To sit down and discuss economics, it would be extremely difficult to prove. Yet, from the standpoint of an audience, *Fortune* magazine once had an article about Farm Holiday Association. It said something like this: "I looked like a school teacher, but don't let it fool you, there are few people who can move an audience as well as he can." A description of me. And I must have been able to because pretty much everything we set out to do we did.

Do you consider yourself an orator?

No. I think of myself something like this complex thing put together, and to use oratory to move people without thinking, I'm absolutely opposed to it. Because what you do with it is not derived from logic and thinking, and it is purely emotional. It's so easy to be wrong. Most of the problems of humanity almost all derive from the fact that we don't do what we ought to do when we ought to do it. Until it becomes so bad that emotion takes over. Then we push the pendulum clear over to the other side.

That's really where you see Milo Reno then?

Yes, that's right. He was using an emotional way. He was an orator.

Do you think that the leadership in the Holiday Movement, particularly in Minnesota, was a steadying influence on the mass of farmers? Were some of the farmers more willing to use violence and did you have to restrain them?

There were those. And I do think that if we had wanted to, we could have had a tremendous amount of violence.

The farmers would have supported more direct action than the leaders advocated?

I don't think there is any question about that.

Do you feel that you always had your hand on the pulse of that leadership, or on that population, or did you feel they were more intense and ahead of your people?

There never was anything about which I felt; here's what I conclude. When I would call a meeting of Harry Haugland and Merle Porter, and George Windingstad, Johnson, about a dozen people. We'd sit down and we might be there 24 hours later talking the thing through, as to what we ought to do, how we ought to do it.

You felt through them, through the local chapter county people, you really did have your hand on the pulse?

I think so.

Much more so than other states did?

Very, very much so. And if you look at what was done it was pretty much what this group felt ought to be done. It didn't arrive from somewhere else.

Shover criticizes the national movement in its earlier years, because the leadership was not in contact, or didn't seem to be in contact, or had lost the discipline of the membership. That doesn't seem to be the picture you feel that Minnesota had?

As far as Milo Reno is concerned, again, I don't want to say something derogatory, because I do feel instinctively he

JOHN BOSCH

wanted to be for the people, he wanted them to be fulfilled, etc. But I don't think that he had any knowledge of history. I don't think he had any knowledge of economics, and what I think he did was to find the heat of the pulse and ride it. I think this is because... look at what happened. Here was Huey Long getting all kinds of publicity. "Could I use Huey Long?" So he was the speaker, or he used Father Coughlin.

Reno wanted to go along with the Long and Coughlin group. How do you estimate the general mass of the farmers would react to this? Were they anti-Long? Would they have followed Reno?

If it would have been possible to get the people with whom I was close to support Milo Reno in what he was trying to do, whether we could have done it, I don't know.

Your own inclinations were not in that direction?

No.

You opposed going with Long.

Here was an emotional climate which somebody was riding. If it wasn't Huey Long, it would be somebody else. There was Father Coughlin riding the monetary issue, investing in silver hoping that he'd get a bi-approach, gold and silver, and he would become extremely wealthy. Somehow, I don't feel, the group didn't feel that this is what we were interested in.

I would question the reaction of the Holiday Movement to the New Deal. What New Deal programs do you think really aided agriculture the most?

I don't think that the New Deal did anywhere near what it could have done nor what it should have done.

Was that Henry Wallace's fault?

I knew Henry Wallace before he became Secretary of Agriculture. His solution... when we were trying to build the Farm Holiday Association he was on some of the committees.

He was one of the early organizers?

Yes. I remember one time when he gave a speech—what we were doing was rabble rousing—he said we should do something to catch the imagination of the people. And if we could get every farmer that raised corn to take a wagonload of corn and put it on the highway and burn it, the fires and smoke rising out through the prairie, this would surely impress the people. I became quite well acquainted with him. He had a home somewhere near Colorado Springs. Every once in awhile he would get people together to spend a weekend to discuss. I was invited there several times and also to Washington. The only thing was that I was the only one who paid my own expenses. I did not want to be in a position to be influenced by somebody paying my expenses. I feel about Henry Wallace, too, that emotionally he wanted everybody to be fulfilled and happy. At the same time, I think he was anything but an orderly coordinated thinker. We never got into any quarrels.

Do you think that the New Deal should have moved towards a more rigid production to keep prices up?

I've never felt that we've had a good farm program, although I think it's better than it would have been than completely without controls whatsoever. We got together with thirteen governors in Des Moines. I remember the meeting very well. Floyd Olson was there, he was chairman of the meeting. We put together a farm program on which all thirteen of the governors concurred. We had a tentative agreement, not a signed agreement, that they would present this agreement to the President, on which they agreed. These thirteen states controlled the food production of the U.S., roughly 90%. And the governors would come together and work with us, declaring a complete stop of the flow of farm commodities until we got it. We spent about a week together putting this program together.

I remember one morning that the closest friend of Milo Reno. . . fellow's name was L. M. Peek, later became president of Farmers Union Life Insurance company, of which Reno was president. Sunday morning was the final morning, and the governors had drafted the proposal and they were going to read it to us in preparing to going to Washington to meet with the President. They had made the appointment. Peek comes in, it's in the wintertime, he has his overcoat in his hand, and as he sits down he throws his overcoat on his seat and a pint of whiskey flew out of the pocket and flew up on the stage, just broke right in front of the governors.

Governor Floyd Olson talked to the President, told him what the program was, had an agreement by telephone that he would help them get it. So they all went to Washington, a committee of five: Olson, Langer, Schmedeman, Herring, and Berry. They went to the White House first, called Wallace and told him they would help them get this. They stayed there. About the third day they thought they were getting a run-around, so they went back to the White House. Floyd Olson told me this. Here they were, all back around the table of the President. The President had promised to help get it over the telephone. So they said we're getting the run-around. "We're governors. We're not just some lobbyists, we are entitled to motion on this thing, and we want to make headway."

The President said, "I'm sorry. I've committed myself to something I can't help you get."

Bill Langer brought his big fists down on the table and he said, "Goddamn it we voted one son-of-a-bitch out of here, and we can do it again" [laughter].

Here was a given farmer. The nature of his farming depends where it is, the size of the farm, the nature of the soil, the family, etc. But a crop in a given year can be wiped out in half an hour or by a drought. That year he doesn't have the surplus, he doesn't have anything. But take year by year, with an average year we are producing more than we are consuming. This is a problem. So, today the federal government pays out billions of dollars to hire farmers not to produce—taking acreage out of production—in addition pays millions and billions of dollars to store the surplus. Just from the standpoint, if you didn't apply it to agriculture, to pay somebody not to do something, while you're not paying him for what he does. If you can think of anthing more asinine than that, I can't.

Two years ago—and I've been trying to get the copy of the newspaper, but I haven't succeeded—the University of Minnesota gets the income tax reports from a number of farmers. They agree that they will not divulge their names or anthing relative to it. Now of the people that do report in that particular year, more than 20% had a cash income of less than $900. Here's investment, total family working, and they have income of less than $900. Who in the hell is weeping and bleeding all over the landscape for those people who are working so hard and get $900? Nobody! Yet we pay billions of dollars to people who don't produce anything.

So, what I proposed then, and I still do ... whatever you want to say, the amount of income a person ought to have when he puts in a full year of work with his investments, say $5,000. This farmer is not contributing to the surplus. He is supporting himself. But supposing that I'm one of the great big ones, and in the things that are being produced, we have 10% too much. Okay, I've got to keep 10%, that's my problem. I produced it, I have to store it, not you. How long will I keep on producing 10% too much? Well, maybe five years, because then I have a guarantee that if I have a bad year I will still have a full crop. But let the guy who has the surplus pay for the surplus, and pay the guy who works for what he does. Now, to pay a family with an investment, with the whole family working $900 a year...as far as I'm concerned that's a crime. How simple is that relative to what we do? How much does it cost? 10, 15 billion dollars, to pay people not to do something. If this isn't idiotic, I don't know what is.

At the University of Minnesota, Walter Heller—there was another one [an economist]—anyway, he was about to go to Washington, and the newspapers were making a big thing about it, so I called him. It was about the farm program. I asked him if he would meet with me to discuss it. We discussed it on the telephone. It was in connection with what they're doing now. We pay people millions of dollars not to produce. We don't pay those who do. We argued about half and hour. Finally he said, "Mr. Bosch, sometimes you have to do what you can do because you can't do what you ought to do."

I said, "Let's put together an audience of a hundred people and you argue your proposition—we have to do what we can do, because we can't do what we ought to do—and I will argue what we ought to do. I'll be you, if you want to bet, that I'll get the majority of the votes. I dare you."

He said, "I've got to go, I've got an appointment at the barber." This was the thing I used to argue with Henry Wallace and the different people he had with him. I always got pretty much the same point.

One of the things which I had a fair amount to do with was to develop the philosophy of profit-sharing in industry. I helped set up the first profit-sharing plant in this part of the United States with the Hormel Packing Company. Very simple. Going back through the record, we found that 80% of the income went to employees, and 20% to management. The plan said we will pay a scale for the industry, but if at the end of the year this is less than 80%, you will get the balance. A few years later, I was a guest of *Fortune* magazine for ten days at

Atlantic City, and Hormel was the other guest from this state. Hormel and I were guests from Minnesota. Two from each state. I asked him how it was working? He said, if I'd been the most selfish man in the world I couldn't have thought of anything better. He said it used to be that if a man was triming too deep or slowing down the line and we tried to discipline the man, we got trouble. But let somebody try it now, and he's out on his ear by the rest of the people on the line. The average income in Hormel and Wilson . . . about 30 miles apart, then they buy in the same area, sell in the same area, Wilson in one, Hormel the other. The employees since that time have averaged $1000 more a year at Hormel than they have at Wilson because the more they do, the more they get.

Well, I helped to invent profit-sharing plans. Somebody in Florida got the same idea. I don't know if you've ever heard of the tax-sheltered salary savings pension plan and trust. That is the name that the IRS gave to them under the terms of which an employee may serve on a tax free basis, what he's earning now. And if he does, the employer must contribute to the fund. Social Security is put together as statistics. The average person begins to earn between 18 and 25. And between that time and 65 you take 100 people and follow them through to 65, one is reasonably well to do. Four have enough to live on, five are still working, 34 are dead and 56 are dead broke . . . not because they didn't earn, but because they didn't save. Well, this plan says to the employee, if you don't care enough for you, to so something for you, how the hell can you ask someone else to do it for you? So we generally put in the plan, if you save 4%, the company has to immediately put in 25% of whatever you do. Well, the man starts out at the age of 20—and this is an easier figure, and is an exaggeration—but say he starts out at age 20 and he's earning $10,000 and you think in terms of 3% of the rate of capital gain or inflation and 7% as the rate of earning and growth of the money. He will have a quarter of a million dollars when he reaches 65. How much will he have otherwise? Well 56% of them won't have anything. That's why I say we don't do what we ought to do when we ought to do it. And pretty soon we do something that brings us clear over to the other side.

Arthur just wants to ask about the relation; did you know Townley?

Yes.

He's interested in this relation of the old Non-Partisan League to the Holiday Movement if there is any. I found a note that said that A.C. Townley in 1923 organized a National Producer's Alliance, and one of the proposals was determining a cost of production and demanding a return of this cost of production, plus a reasonable profit. Is that where Farm Holiday got some of its ideas?

No. If it did at that particular time I never heard of it. The cost of production idea as far as I'm concerned originated with Ed Kennedy, who was secretary of the National Farm Union Organization. He put together a big mass of figures. Later he became involved in something much ... as far as he was concerned, his personal habits got him out of the picture. He was a bright boy.

What year did Ed Kennedy put this together?

About the same time that Roosevelt became President.

'32?

Around that area. We used his figures for cost of production in the Farm Holiday Association presentation. But A.C. Townley was going to become wealthy growing flax. He went broke, Later on, my father was a lifetime member in the Non-Partisan League. But when the Farm Holiday Association started, A.C. Townley and the Non-Partisan League had been pretty much discredited. The Farmer's Labor Party, later became the DFL of the Democratic Party. Floyd Olson became head of it. Between the two of them, I knew them both quite well. Floyd Olson was miles above A.C. Townley. He was quite an orator.

He [Townley] went to the state capitol, told Floyd Olson that I had asked him to come and wanted Floyd Olson to help him finance the building of a paper, the *Farm Holiday News.* Floyd Olson did. It just never occured to him that he might be lying about the thing. I don't know if he thought about me having an alliance with A.C. Townley or what. After he got his commitment, he came out to the farm. He stopped in. He said, "You know, it's kind of funny; here I've been working on this thing all the time, and here you get out on the arm, you almost took it away from me." He said, "I've made it up with Floyd Olson, and now I'm the head of it. I've got the newspaper and I'll do with it what I damn please." A Farm Holiday associate, and he told me this, and I was the guy that started it.

We had a special meeting of the Farm Holiday Association in Des Moines, Iowa. A.C. Townley had come up with an idea that the Farm Holiday Association should make an alliance with the CIO and we'd take over the country. You know something, he sold this to Milo Reno. He was the speaker at this meeting. I wasn't feeling very happy. The whole thing had gone haywire. Finally, I got to see Townley with his supporters in the room—I had my supporters—and I said, "I'll make a deal with you. We won't fight you when you present this to the convention tomorrow. We'll authroize you to speak for the Farm Holiday Association, but you will sign an agreement that the newspaper is mine." So we made the deal, and we signed it that night.

The next day he was giving his oration and he knew he wasn't making any headway, and the less headway the more he talked. Different people would come up to me and say "Stop the son-of-a-bitch; stop the son-of-a-bitch," and I could see that the more he talked the less he was making. And even Milo Reno, who was the one to whom he sold the idea under whose auspices he was presenting this. This was in an auditorium, and they were doing some repair work, and there was a piece of 2x4, about that long, and Milo Reno goes over and picks it up and brings it over to the table and Wham he damn near broke the table [Laughter]. Well, anyway I got up and said, "Let's not make an issue of this, but a simple resolution. We'll authorize Mr. Townley to go to the CIO convention, and make his presentation, and prepare a paragraph or two that we authorize him to do it." This was done; on that basis the Farm Holiday newspaper becomes mine. That's what we did. That's the last we ever heard of him.

Where in your background, formal training or what, do you credit this political gift that you have?

My father was an unusual person. As I mentioned there were fourteen children in the family, seven girls and seven boys. What do you do in the winter time? Well, we picked a topic and we'd debate it. But the next Saturday we had to take the opposite side. Son of a gun, that's good. Really—to be able to look at a question from different sides. There aren't too many people who could do it. My education, if you can call it education; I went to rural eighth grade. I never had a chance to go to high school. I married fairly young.

Did you ever think that you would classify yourself as a radical?

It's a question that I've debated, frankly. I'd like to use two terms, conservative and progressive. I suppose that any one would say that you were for progress. You may not agree to what is progress, and you certainly could disagree as to what produces progress. But I doubt whether any one would say that he's not for progress. The question is, how to define it. How do we produce it? I think it's highly debatable and ought to be. Conservative—what do you want to conserve?

When do you want to conserve it? How do you go about conserving it? As far as I'm concerned those things which did produce progress at best, those are the things I want to conserve.

Change, in and of itself, is not necessarily good. It's a hell of a lot easier to change for the worse than it is for the better. As witness, some 22 civilizations which grew and died. I think we are at a critical stage in the history of the human race right now. I suppose you've read Erick Hoffer considerably; he doesn't write anymore. Recently retired. I don't say that I agree with everything that he said, but I do feel this: the function of education, religion, society—the function of all this should be to, to permit an individual to be his best, to cause him to be his best. These are the two things that I think are important. All our philosophy should be aimed in that direction, and there is a vast difference in people. There are those who do it instinctively, and there are those who do as little as they are permitted to do. And the more you do for those who could do it for themselves, the less they will do for themselves. The best athlete, after he's spent a couple years in bed, is crippled. As I see it, the function of the total environment should be to cause the individual to be his best. This is the thing I've tried to do.

After these some forty years with the Farm Holiday Association, what should we really learn from those years and those activities of the Farm Holiday Association?

What one generation learns, does not mean the next generation inherits. They may have to learn over again.

INDEX

Adrian (MN) 127
Aetna Life Insurance Company, 132, 136
Alexandria (MN), 116
Allendorf (IA), 57
American Manufacturers Association, 194
Anderson, Paul (Sheriff), 93, 164, 186, 187
Anoka (MN), 164
Appleton (MN), 6, 20
Associated Farmers of Iowa, 21
Atwater (MN), **xviii, 92, 94**
Attorneys, 16, 123
Augeson, O.B., 11
Bank Holiday, 40, 182
Banker's Life Mortgage Company, 29
Barkus, Carl, 189, 190
Bemidji (MN), 121
Benson, Elmer (Governor), 19, 28, 70, 135-36, 165, 200
Bergen Creamery (Jackson, MN), 76, 77
Berry, XXXX (Governor of SD), 207
Bigelow (MN), 128, 129
Big Stone County, 20
Bridges, Harry, 200
Birnie, Mrs., 157
Bolman, Elmer, 8
Bosch, John, **xviii, xx, xxix**, 10, 15, 46, 71, 90, 92, 100-102, 124, 140-141, 151, 157-15, 163, 167, 180-214
Bosch, Herbert, 163-164, 187
Bosch, Richard, 163-202
Brecht, Arnold, 69
Brumel, XXXX, 74
Buffalo (MN), 138
Butz, Earl, 85
California, 134
Canby (MN), xxii, 66, 85, 177
Chicago (ILL), 155
Chippewa County (MN), **xix, xxii, xxvi**, 2, 8, 9-10, 72, 188, 189
Clarkfield (MN), 172, 178
Clay County (MN), 100
Cook County (ILL), 134
Cooperatives, 137, 183
Coughlin, Father, 191, 196, 205
commodity prices, xi, 39, 43, 49, 60, 68, 105, 118, 134, 138, 139, 149, 155, 175, 181, 193

Commons, John R., 202
Commonwealth College (ARK), 202
cost of production, xvii, 13, 46, 91, 168, 170, 182
Craft, William, 51
CWA, 40
Davis, John I., 7
Davis, Tom, 69
Des Moines (IA), xii, 183, 206
Devel County (SD), 69
Donaldson's Department Store, 5, 90
Duford, XXXX, 122
Dyson, Lowell, xxix
Ebeling, Louis, 127-130
Echo (MN), 111
Engebretson, John, 145-148
ever-normal granary, 17
Fairmont (MN), 51
Farm Bureau, xviii, xxi, xxiv, 27, 36, 47, 79, 134, 148
Farm Holiday News, 212
Farmer-Labor Party, 1, 19, 21, 39, 45, 64
Farmer's Labor Party, 211
Farmer's National Committee for Action
Farmers Union, xxi-xxiii, xxvi, xviii, 2, 25-27, 29, 31, 45, 47, 49, 51, 59, 62-63, 78, 90, 133, 141, 142, 148, 165, 182, 186
Farmers' Holiday Association
    boycotts of produce (produce withholding), xii, xiii-xv, xvii, xix, xx 22, 27, 48-50, 75-77, 79, 96, 87-98, 105, 125, 137-138, 152, 165, 184-186, 206-207
    communist influences (alleged), xxiv, xxvi, xxix, 42, 62-63, 80, 117, 142, 157, 199-200
    debt adjustment committees, xvii, 4, 16, 29, 52, 73, 93, 145-146, 160-162
    dues 14, 81, 92, 196
    fascist influences (alleged), 12, 25, 165
    march in St. Paul, MN (March 22, 1933), xxvi, 81-82, 117-118, 139-140, 154
    meetings, 15, 47, 49, 73, 75, 90, 91-92, 125, 169, 178, 204, 212-13
    membership, 3, 14, 26, 49, 53, 59-60, 67, 83, 99-100, 121, 185
    mortgage foreclosure sales, xv-xvi, xxi-xxiii, 3, 15, 22, 31-33, 49-53, 57, 65, 72, 93-94, 109-112, 115, 116, 121-123, 127-128, 132, 133, 145, 164, 172, 173, 186-192, 199
    national conventions, 11-13, 183, 197-199
    organization of, xx, 2, 5-6, 29, 47, 52-53, 60-61, 75, 92, 149, 151, 170, 184-186, 198-199, 204, 206
    public reaction to, xix, xx, xxiv-xxv, 31, 38, 47, 50, 58-59, 58, 78, 98, 99, 114, 152, 165, 167

INDEX 217

    state conventions, 11-12
    travel, xx, 8, 45-46, 57, 80, 90-91, 100, 197
    violence and potential for violence, 3, 8, 9, 31-33, 55, 57, 66, 79, 82, 84, 86-88, 94, 95, 96, 106, 123, 124, 126, 150, 151, 152, 159, 165-166, 174, 177, 190, 192-193, 203-204
    women's involvement in, **xxviii, 8, 83-84, 95**
Federal Debt Conciliation Commission Act, 194, 195
Federal Land Bank, 6, 7, 10, 29, 52, 111, 112, 128, 194
Federal Reserve System, 182
Felt, Ruben, 90
foreclosure sale (see Farmers' Holiday Association. mortgage foreclosure sales)
Fortune Magazine, 203, 209
Fry, XXXX, 73-74
Ghandi, xx, 201-202
Goede, William, 45-53, 79
Gold, D. W., 108-114
Grain Terminal Association, 13
Grange, **xii, xiv**
Granite Falls (MN), 67, 71, 110, 172
Habbick, XXXX, 58
Hacker, George, 7
Hanson, Soren, **xxii**
Haraldson, Maynard, 90
Haroldson, Clinton, 89-104, 165
Harris, Lem, 199
Haugland, Harry, 8, 10, 92, 141-142, 188, 189, 204
Heller, Walter, 209
Heron Lake (MN), 51, 86
Herring, XXXX (Governor of IA), 207
Hicks, John, xxxii
Highway Patrol, 9
Hillman, William, 90
Hoffer, Erick, 214
Hofstadter, Richard, **xxvii, xxx**
Hoover, Herbert, xiv, xvii, 88
Hormel Packing Company, xx   209-210
Howard Lake, xx
Humphrey, Hubert H., 13
Idaho, 62-63
Insurance Companies, xxi   3, 6, 9, 11, 16, 30, 33, 41-42, 49-52, 108-113, 121, 129, 132, 136, 153, 160, 174, 195
Iowa, **xi, xvi, xviii, xxv,** 74, 84, 106, 152, 157, 184, 187, 188, 196
Ivanhoe (MN), 33, 115, 116, 118, 189
Jackson (MN), 48, 75, 76, 79, 80
Jackson County (MN), 73, 75, 84, 122, 151-153

Johnson, Charles, 49, 75, 76, 79, 80
Johnson, E., 73-88
Johnson, William, 115-119
Joint Stock Land Bank, 108
Kanabec County (MN), 100
Kandiyohi County (MN), xviii, xix, xxi, 71, 89, 91, 92, 93, 96, 112, 182, 183, 186, 188, 189
Kenneth (MN), 147
Kimball Township (MN), 53
Kramer, Dale, xxxi
Lac Qui Parle County (MN), xix, xxii, xxiv, 2, 94, 115, 188
Lake Benton (MN), 22, 30
Lake Elizabeth (MN), 182, 186, 187
Lakefield, 45, 48, 49, 51, 75, 76
Lake Lillian Township (MN), 90, 93, 164, 167
Lake Wilson (MN), 118
Langer, William, 185, 191, 207
Lawson, Victor, 11
Lee, Robert E., 186
LeMars (IA), 79
Lemke, William, 191, 199
Lincoln County (MN), xxiv, 22, 24, 29, 69, 115
Little Falls (MN), 91
Local 574 (Teamsters), 5, 185
Long, Huey, 12, 196, 205
Lund, Clarence, 163-169
Lund, Guy, 22-37
Lundeen, Ernie, 20
Luoma, Everett, xxix
Lyon County (MN), 55, 65, 69, 72
Madison (MN), 72, 74
Mankato (MN), 10
Marshall (MN), 8, 39, 42, 55, 171, 175-177, 184
Mattson, Axel, 137-143
McGinnis, XXXX, 122
McGowan, John, 20
Meehl, David, 65-72
Milbank (SD), 31
Minneapolis, 128, 129, 156, 185, 195
Minneapolis Tribune, 6
Minneapolis Star, 165
Minneapolis Law Enforcement League, 69
Montevideo (MN), xix, xx, 67, 72, 91, 137, 177, 194
Moratorium (federal) on foreclosures, xvi, 40-42, 86, 103, 124, 153, 176, 182, 191, 195
Morlan, Robert, xxxii

INDEX

Mountain Lake (MN), 75, 149
Murphy, Frank, 16
Mutual Benefit Life Insurance Company, 108, 111, 112
National Farm Credit Administration, 52
National Farm Organization (NFO), 2, 27, 67, 167
National Guard, 5, 47, 173
National Producer's Alliance, 211
Nebraska, 191
Nelson, Hemming, 45-46, 90, 181
Nelson, Nels, 165
New Deal, xii, xvi, xvii, xxvii, xxix, **205, 206**
Newspapers, 6, 11, 78, 82, 121
Nicollet Hotel, 200
Nobles County (MN), xxi, 57, 59, 60, 69, 145
Non-Partisan League, xiv, 1, 20, 35, 49, 121, 123, 145, 159, 211
Nordin, D. Sven, xxx
North Dakota, 90, 123, 171, 185, 187, 190, 191, 195
Norwest Mortgage & Trust, 41
Nystrom, William, 57-64, 78
Oklahoma City, 183
Olivia (MN), 111, 116
Olson, David, 149-162
Olson, Floyd (Governor), **xxii, xxvii,** 16, 19, 21, 39, 51, 52, 56, 64, 70, 75, 85-88, 102, 107, 116, 117-118, 124, 135, 137, 139-140, 151, 154-155, 161, 168, 169, 185, 186, 189, 190, 191-194, 207, 212
Olson, George, 77, 151
Olson, Harry, 77
Olson, I.O., 58
Omaha (NB), 105, 184
Organizing farmers, 60-61
Ortonville (MN), 8, 20
Peek, L.M., 207
Penny auctions, **xvi, xxiii,** 8, 23, 52, 57, 73-75, 87, 93, 95, 132, 137, 150-151, 174, 186
Perry, Frank, 6, 8, 15, 16
Peters, Peter, 127
Peterson, Allenson, 11
Peterson, Harold, 90, 91
Peterson, Nordahl, xxii
Peterson, Roy, 1-21
Philbrick, Herbert, 62
Porter, Merle, 8, 188, 189, 204
Prudential Insurance Company, 121-123
PWA, 40, 43
Railroads, 13, 20
Reading (MN), 127

Reno, Milo, **xxi, xiii, xvi, xviii, xxix,** 3, 17, 80, 102, 141, 183, 196, 197, 203, 204-205, 207, 212
Renville County (MN), 2, 111
Rochester (MN), 108
Roots of Reform, 188
Roosevelt, F.D., **xv, xvi, xxv, 3, 4, 5, 6, 17, 70, 82, 142, 143, 155, 172,** 175, 189, 189, 193, 206-207
Ross, Louis, 58
Rowe, Eldon, 106
Rushmore (SD), 127, 128
Saloutos, Theodore, xxix, xxxi, xxxii
Schapsmeier, Edward and Fredrick, xxxi
Schmedeman, Albert G., (governor of WI), 207
Sheriffs, 9, 23, 29, 31, 52, 55, 65, 66, 74, 79, 85, 87, 93, 106, 110, 111, 112, 115, 151, 152-153, 172, 174, 175, 186, 190, 191
Shoemaker, Francis, 47
Shover, John, xxix,
Siebring, XXXX, 71
Sioux City (IA), xv, xvi, 17, 105, 184
Sioux Falls (SD), 131
Slot machines, 92
Smalgaard, XXXX, 188
South Dakota, 132
South St. Paul, 137, 139, 184
Spirit Lake, 48
Staley, Oren Lee, 2
Stassen, Harold, 71
St. Cloud (MN), xx
St. James (MN), 73-74
St. Leo (MN), 170
St. Paul (MN), 185, 197
Stocklan, XXXX, 164
Stonstegard, Goody, 43
Stover, Fred, 21
Superior National Forest, 43
Supreme Court (of U.S.), 75, 86
Svea (MN), 90
Swift County (MN), 2, 5, 6, 8, 12, 16-17, 20, 132
Swift County Bank, 16
Swift & Company (Marshall, MN), 39, 65-57, 176
Tatge, O., 131-136
Thatcher, M.W., 13
Thomas, Ben, 187
Thompson, Gordon, 105-107
Tkach, Andrew, 121-126
Torkelson, Chris, 128, 129

INDEX

Townley, A.C., 80, 211, 212
Trimont (MN), 149
Tyler (MN), 30
Union Central Railroad, 9-10
United Farmer's League, 199-200
U.S. Marshalls, 9, 10-11, 72, 94, 192
Walker (MN), 91-92
Wallace, Henry, xvi, xxix, **17, 194, 205, 206, 207, 209**
Waltersdorf, Matt, 128
Washington, D.C., xix, 57-59, 140-141, 155, 171, 206, 207
Watonwan County (MN), 73-74, 84
Wefald, Jon, **xxvii**
West Central Tribune, 11
White, Roland, **xxix**
Wiebe, Robert, **xxx**
Williams, M.F., 110
Willmar (MN), xxi, 11, 89, 93, 96, 116, 167, 182, 187
Wilmont (MN), 128
Windingstad, George, 188, 190, 204
Windom (MN), 48, 69, 76
Winslow, C.A., 188
Wolf, Henry, 8
Wolf, Laura, 8
Wood Lake (MN), 109
World War I, 114
World War II, 17, 35, 104
Worthington (MN), xxi, 48, 58, 78, 107, 171, 184
Yellow Medicine County (MN), 72, 110-111, 115, 188
Ziebarth, E.W., 189
Zoic, William, 202